MW00642081

ויהי בנסוע הארון

ויהי בנסוע הארון

SEVENTY CONVERSATIONS
in Transit with HaGaon HaRav
JOSEPH B. SOLOVEITCHIK *zt"l*

AARON ADLER

Spiritual Leader, Ohel Nechama Community Synagogue,
Katamon, Jerusalem

Founding Rosh Yeshiva, Yeshivat Bnei Akiva, Ner Tamid
Hashmona'im

OUPRESS

ORTHODOX UNION PRESS
New York

URIM PUBLICATIONS
Jerusalem • New York

ויהי בנסוע הארון

Seventy Conversations in Transit
with HaGaon HaRav Joseph B. Soloveitchik *zt"l*

by Aaron Adler

Typeset by Ariel Walden

Printed in Israel

First Edition

ISBN 978-1-60280-424-1

Urim Publications
P.O. Box 52287,
Jerusalem 9152102
Israel

www.UrimPublications.com

Orthodox Union Press
11 Broadway,
New York, NY 10004
USA

www.ou.org

Library of Congress Cataloging-in-Publication Data in progress.

*D*edicated with esteem, honor
and deep respect

To my brother

RABBI YOSEF ADLER

Spiritual Leader, Congregation Rinat Yisrael, Teaneck, NJ
Rosh Yeshiva, Torah Academy of Bergen County, Teaneck, NJ

Serving as my role model in many of life's endeavors throughout my formative years, Yossi, as he is known affectionately
by family and friends, personifies the ideal blend of rabbinic
inspiration, coupled with educational excellence – exemplified
by our Rebbe, the Rav *zt"l.*

84 Bennett Avenue
New York, New York 10033
(212) 795-0630

הרב צבי שכטר
רב ביהמ"ד · שבת ורמב"ם
ישיבת רבינו יצחק אלחנן

<u>מכתב ברכה —</u>

בשמחה רבתי וגו' פ[...] הנחמא [...]
כ"ג יקירי הרה"ג הרב ר' אהרן [...] שליט"א
אשר שמח, וורד' [...]
נבונים [...] הא שמחה. [...]
הספרא ד' [...] על עבודת [...]
אגרדים משמע ע[...] לה[...]
[...] קרן לו, [...]
אין הספר, כי [...] ע[...] ה[...]
ו[...] עיני הספר [...] שלמ[...]
הרה"ג המחבר [...] שית [...]
[...] ה [...] הרא[...]

בברכת
שלי [...]
אוהבו [...]
[...]

Rabbi Herschel Shachter
24 Bennett Avenue
New York, New York 10033
(212) 795–0630

Letter of *Berakha*

On Shabbat, I had the opportunity of reviewing the delight-
ful Sefer of my dear [student], R' Aharon Shlomo Adler, ויהי
בנסוע הארון, which I thoroughly enjoyed. My Shabbat, *Parshat
Zakhor*, was transformed into a Shabbat of sweet memories
of the past years. It appears to me that all those who studied
with the Rav *z"l* will enjoy this sefer, for it encompasses both
Halakhic issues as well as issues of Hashkafa. We extend our
gratitude to the author for committing to writing all [of these
conversations].

Respectfully,
[R' Hershel] Tzvi Schachter
Motza'ei Shabbat,
Parshat Zakhor, 5780

Contents

Dedication   5
Letter of *Berakha*   7
Preface   13

I. Halakhic Decisions and Reasoning

1. Rendering Halakhic Decisions Appropriately   27
2. Strictness and Leniency in Cases of Doubt   30
3. Prenatal Testing   32
4. Treating a Cerebral Death Patient   34
5. Loss of Mucus Plug   36
6. Celebrating Thanksgiving Day   37
7. Standing Up at a *Zimun* of Ten   39
8. *Zimun* for Women   40
9. Ten Women for *Megillah* Reading   42
10. Repeating Two Verses in *Megillah* Reading   44
11. Family Grave Visitations   45
12. *Tevilat Keilim* for Electrical Appliances   47
13. Replacing Vacuum Cleaner Bags before Pesah   48
14. Purchasing *Hametz* Products after Pesah   50
15. Shabbat Candles in Homes of Others   52
16. Hanukah Candles in Modern Times   53
17. Torah Reading Outside the Framework of Prayer   55
18. "Glatt Kosher Meat"   56
19. *Gomel* Blessing for Air Travel   58
20. No "Amen" Response after *Gomel* Blessing   60

Contents

II. Teaching Torah

21. On Being Referred to as "The Rav" 67
22. Down to Earth Rabbis and Educators 69
23. Versatility in Teaching 70
24. Ingredients for a Good *Shiur* 71
25. Elevating the Mediocre Students 73
26. Educating Towards *Aliya* to Israel 75
27. Educating the Non-Religious Students 76
28. Unpublished Books 79
29. Perseverant to Understand 81
30. Inquiry from my Younger Brother 83
31. Mundane Talk 84
32. Torah Study Can Take Place Anywhere 86
33. Positive Evil Inclinations 87
34. Torah Education for Women 89
35. My Driver Asked ... 93

III. Israel and the Jewish Nation

36. *Aliya* Discussions 101
37. *Hallel* on Yom Ha'Atzmaut – an Official Position 105
38. Reacting to Menachem Begin's Election (1977) 108
39. The 1977 Rav/Menachem Begin Meeting 109
40. Rejecting Chief Rabbi of Israel Offer 111
41. Issue of "Who is a Jew" 113
42. Vote for Gerald Ford (1976) 115
43. Blessing to the Newly-Elected President of Mizrahi 116
44. The Joseph Gruss Connection 118
45. Soviet Jewry Rallies 123

IV. Integrity and Sensitivity

46. The Gruenspecht Family *Shiva* Visit 127
47. Limits on *Mesirah* Prohibition 129
48. Operating a Yeshiva without Government Funding 131
49. Business Ethics 132
50. Consolation after Car Stolen 134
51. Bedside Prayer for Dr. Belkin 135
52. Blessings Received from an Ordinary Person 138
53. Throwing in the Towel and Attitude toward Painkillers 139

V. Personal Conduct and Relationships

54. The Hassidic and the Mussar Movements   143
55. A Humble Disposition   145
56. The Two Hayims of the 19th Century   147
57. The Rav and the Rebbe in Berlin   148
58. The 1980 Visit to 770   150
59. Shabbat Candles for Young Girls   152
60. Private Conversations with a Dutch Cardinal   154
61. Strict Behavior Recommendations   156
62. Wedding Gift and Advice   158
63. No Laziness on the Rabbinic Watch   159
64. Entering the Rabbinate   160
65. Eulogizing Unknown People   162
66. Charity and Philanthropic Activities   163
67. The Yeshiva University Cafeteria   167
68. Returning a Nickel; Refunding Parking & Toll Fees   169
69. Rav's Two Allergic Reactions   171
70. Epilogue – My Final Conversation (1985)   173

Postscript   177

Preface

The Talmud (*Berakhot* 7b) relates that "Attending to one's teacher of Torah is more meritorious than studying under him" גדולה שימושה של תורה יותר מלימודה –. This work is a compilation of seventy edited conversations conducted between our great Rebbe, *HaGaon HaRav* Joseph B. Soloveitchik *zt"l* (1903–1993) and me predominantly while in transit. "The Rav," as he was popularly known (see Conversation #21), arguably one of the master disseminators of Torah of the twentieth century,[1] trained over two thousand Rabbis in nearly half a century of teaching at the Rabbi Isaac Elchanan Theological Seminary (1941–1986) affiliated with Yeshiva University (YU). The Rav's son-in-law, R' Prof. Yitzhak Twersky *zt"l*, referred to him as "the Rambam of our generation."[2] The Rav's biography has been chronicled several times over during his lifetime as well as posthumously. In 2006, a full-length documentary film was produced and directed by Ethan Eisenberg entitled: The Lonely Man of Faith.[3]

---

1. See *Iggrot Moshe*, YD 3:43, (and again in *Kevod HaRav*, ed. M. Sherman and J. Woolf, 1984) – מרביץ תורה ברבים – an appellation used exclusively by R' Moshe Feinstein for the Rav.

2. See *K'Ma'ayan HaMitgaber*, Hebrew, ed. R' Prof. Carmi Horowitz, 2020, p. 160.

3. For a comprehensive biography of the Rav, see R' Aaron Rakeffet-Rothkoff, in *Emunah Bizmanim Mishtanim*, 1996, pp. 17–41. R' Aharon Lichtenstein, in *Great Jewish Thinkers of the Twentieth Century*, ed. S. Noveck, 1963, pp. 281–297, penned a deeply-insightful biographical analytical essay of his father-in-law, the Rav.

The Rav commuted weekly between his hometown – Boston – and New York City. One could characterize the Rav's rabbinic and teaching years, in the words of the 19th century novelist, Charles Dickens, as "A Tale of Two Cities." In both loci, the Rav was pre-occupied with the teaching and spreading of Torah knowledge and wealth. And, most importantly, in both cities the Rav was appreciated by the masses who attended his various weekly and annual public *Shiurim*. His vast erudition of Torah and general knowledge, along with the gift of his sensational oratorical skills (in both Yiddish and English) mesmerized crowds of thousands who flocked to absorb his thoughts and inspirations. Some of these talks would last four hours!

Yet, the Rav exhibited a dual persona in oscillating weekly between Boston and New York.

In Boston, the Rav functioned as a town Rabbi, generally relaxed and accessible to the general public. Whereas in New York, the Rav exhibited a more stoic "*Rosh Yeshiva*" posture. His very presence in New York – in and out of YU confines – was surrounded by an awe-inspiring spirit of tension.

I vividly recall my first personal encounter with the Rav. We were standing together in a rather full YU elevator. The Rav didn't speak to anyone. Everyone simply froze and stood at attention until the Rav exited the elevator. It was a frightening and awesome experience.

Most New Yorkers who were acquainted with the Rav rarely had the opportunity to engage in private conversations with him. An encounter with the Rav was an exercise in "God fearing" behavior, as dictated by the spirit of the Mishnah, *Avot* 4:12, ומורא רבך כמורא שמים. There was always a perceptible distance between the Rav and all the others. We, in New York, were occasionally jealous of our parallel Bostonians who enjoyed the advantage of the Rav's closeness and attention.[4]

4. See S. Farber, "National and Local Leadership – The Rav's Boston

The tale of two cities was also a story of weekly intercity travel between Boston and New York. During the 1940s and 1950s, the Rav traveled by rail with his wife Tonya *a"h*. However, from the late 1950s through the 1980s, the Rav flew regularly to and from New York on the Eastern Airlines hourly commuter shuttle flights.

During the winter of 1967, the Rav suffered a triple-edged personal blow with the losses of his mother, Pesha nee Feinstein (20 *Tevet*), his brother, Dr. Samuel Soloveitchik (15 *Adar* 1), and – most crushing – his wife, Dr. Tonya nee Lewit (11 *Adar* 2).

It became evident, shortly after the passing of the Rav's wife, that he would require personal assistance while in New York. Thus, the role of the Rav's *Shamash* was created in order to give some sense of order to the Rav's schedule and apartment keeping. The first, Mordechai Fuerstein, was a Bostonian well acquainted with the Rav from his hometown. The next in line was Mark Karasick, who in turn passed it on in 1974 to my older brother, Yosef Adler. It was in September of 1974 that my brother called me one day inviting me to serve as the Rav's personal driver for that year. I recall responding in the affirmative and nearly fainting after hanging up the phone. Although being exposed to the Rav's public *Shiurim* for several years since 1968, this would, nevertheless, be my first official year in the Rav's *Shiur*. Added to this tension would be the task of chauffeuring the Rav every Tuesday morning from LaGuardia Airport to YU, and to be available on Wednesdays for city appointments. (Other drivers took the Rav back to the airport on Thursday afternoons and to/from his weekly Tuesday night Moriah Synagogue *Shiur*.)

Persona" – Hebrew, *HaRav B'Olam HeHadash*, 2010, p. 500. The author speaks of the geographic duality in the Rav's life – acknowledged by the Rav himself – reflecting the tensions between the *Rosh Yeshiva* type and the community Rabbi position. See also, R' Norman Lamm *z"l*, "*Hesped Mar:* A Eulogy for the Rav," *Memories of a Giant*, 2003, p. 223, and R' Mendi Gopin, *Davening with the Rav*, 2006, pg. 15, who writes, "How different he was in Brookline than in New York – much less tense, much more approachable."

As for me, I was thrilled to have this unusual private quality time with the Rav, which continued from 1974–1977. I began fantasizing, somewhat identifying with the Vilna Gaon's wagon driver (בעל עגלה). This was the Rav – one of the greatest Torah personalities of the millennia (!) – sitting to my right in my 1964 Chevrolet while allowing me to talk to him.

Realizing early in the school year that this experience would be a game changer in my life, I began to give serious thought each week regarding the subjects I planned to discuss with him. On a small piece of paper I would write down ten subjects. If, on a given trip, I succeeded in talking to the Rav about three of these subjects, that would be considered a great day. These conversations would take place in transit from the moment of the pickup at the airport until the delivery at YU. (Some of the conversations took place even after our arrival at the Rav's apartment.) This trip should normally have taken approximately fifteen minutes. However, I deliberately drove in the right-hand slow lane in order to squeeze out another five minutes of the Rav's attention.

> Many years later, in 2013, at the twentieth anniversary observance of the Rav's passing in Alon Shevut, the Rav's daughter, Dr. Tova Lichtenstein, remarked to me: we both know that my father was an intelligent man and certainly knew all along exactly what you were doing. Yet, he never said a word to you about those extra minutes with him.

These private discussions focused upon various areas of concern. We talked about Halakhic issues on both the theoretical and practical levels. We conversed about issues related to Jewish current events both in the United States as well as in Israel. Practical educational issues were high on my agenda. The Rav patiently listened to my novel homiletic interpretations, while, all along I was polishing my sermonic skills. The Rav showed interest in the progress of my M.A degree dissertation at the Bernard Revel Graduate School (YU) dealing with the contradictions phenomenon between Rambam's Mishnah Commentary and his Mishneh Torah codes.[5] The Rav shared with me personal experiences over the years. And, beyond his sheer genius in Torah, the Rav exemplified the best in moral and ethical behavior. Without question, he served as the absolute role model for me as well as many others, in personal conduct issues.

The preserved seventy edited conversations found in this book have been topically broken down to offer some order to an otherwise non-sequential framework of the various segments. They are arranged according to the following general headings:

I. Halakhic Decisions and Reasoning
II. Teaching Torah
III. Israel and the Jewish Nation
IV. Integrity and Sensitivity
V. Personal Conduct and Relationships

The book's subtitle, *Seventy Conversations in Transit with HaGaon HaRav Joseph B. Soloveitchik zt"l*, describes perfectly the message of the Hebrew title, ויהי בנסוע הארון ("And the Ark traveled"). Playing on the word הארון we have the letters of my name, אהרון. The scene is that of the personification of that ארון housing the whole gamut of Torah while in travel. These experiences with the Rav were in total fulfillment of Torah study "on the way" (ובלכתך בדרך). The Rav, represented by the Temple's

5. See Aaron Adler, "The Relationship of Rambam to the Yerushalmi" (Hebrew), in the *R' Yosef Kafiah Memorial Volume*, 2001, pg. 205, note 20. The Rav commented to me that during the past eight hundred years, the intuition of Torah giants guided them away from expending much intellectual intensity and efforts over the Mishnah Commentary texts – as opposed to the Mishneh Torah codes. The reason being is that the Mishnah Commentary came down in translation from the original Judeo-Arabic, coupled with assorted manuscript corruptions. There was an overall lack of confidence in these texts as to whether or not the "authentic" Rambam was actually being studied.

Ark, was beautifully described by R' Menachem Genack in his Introduction to the Rabbi J.B. Soloveitchik Memorial Issue of *Tradition*, Vol. 30, 1996 (reprinted here with the kind permission of the author):

> The *Aron*, the Holy Ark, had two poles, *badim* with which it was to be carried. Surprising, despite the divine design of the Temple, when the Ark was placed in the Holy of Holies, these two poles, which were never to be removed, were not completely contained within the cubits of the sacred chamber and therefore protruded into the curtain, the *parokhet* which separated the Holy from the Holy of Holies. The Ark containing the Torah was cloistered in the secluded Holy of Holies, where no one, save the High Priest on *Yom Kippur,* may enter. This represents the pristine, unadulterated quality of the Torah. Above the Ark were the *keruvim*, the cherubs, with their childlike faces representing the innocence and purity of Torah. Yet while the Torah must remain pure, undiluted and unchanging as the day when it was plucked from its heavenly abode to be given to man, it must leave the Sanctum Sanctorum to animate all of life outside the protected environment of the Holy of Holies. The *badim* represent the portability of Torah and its significance in all times, circumstances, places and areas of human endeavor. From its protected sacred quarters, the immutable Torah radiates sanctity and meaning to our ever changing lives. From its secluded private realm, which must be guarded and sheltered, the Torah bursts forth to the hurly-burly of the marketplace and public domain.
>
> The Rav, Rabbi Joseph B. Soloveitchik *zt"l*, represented, in his life's work, this dimension of the *Aron*. He protected the integrity of our traditions, both intellectual and practical, from all illicit incursions into the Holy of Holies. But he was not satisfied to live in an ivory tower, isolated from the contemporary scene, for that would have limited the impact, message, and thereby, the grandeur of Torah. He made Torah portable, relevant and alive even in the modern environment, far from the protected existence he had known as a child.

Our Rabbis (*B. Yoma* 54a) interpret the verse, 'My beloved is unto me as a bag of myrrh, that lieth betwixt my breasts' (*Song of Songs* 1:13) as an allusion to the protrusion of the *badim* into the parochet. This represents the eternal, life-giving nourishment which the Torah grants us. So too, were we nourished by the richness of the Rav's personality and erudition, 'as a nursing-father carrieth the suckling child unto the land which thou didst swear unto their father' (*Num.* 11:12).

When Rabbi Yehuda haNasi died, the bitter news was communicated with the metaphor that the Ark had been captured. Rabbi Yehuda, the author of the *Mishna,* who saved Torah in a time of great transition, personified the Torah, the *Aron haKodesh.* Our own rebbe's brilliant life of commitment and devotion in times of great challenge is also personified by the *Aron* – the *Aron* with the *badim.*

The cadre of the Rav's drivers, both in Boston and New York, had the enormous merit (זכות) of fulfilling the mandate of the Levite tribe of old: (Shemot 25:14) – לשאת את הארון – to carry the Ark while in motion. For me, at least, these private conversations with the Rav impacted on my future no less than all the formal *Shiurim* of the Rav that I was privileged to attend – if not more so. Reiterating my opening line from the Talmud, "Attending to one's teacher of Torah is more meritorious than studying under him" – גדולה שימושה של תורה יותר מלימודה.

The gestation period for this book began over forty years ago prior to making *Aliya* to Israel. Already at that early stage, in the name of preserving accuracy, the contents were arranged topically, along with the book's Hebrew name. However, the long incubation period was due to several objective and subjective factors. My rabbinic and educational responsibilities prevented me from properly focusing upon publication of this material. Perhaps, I was partially influenced by the Rav's family "allergy" against the printing press (see Conversation #69). The Rav's first full-length book – an anthology of public addresses on Repentance (על התשובה) – appeared when the Rav was approaching age seventy! In the final analysis, it was the encouragement of many teachers, family members, and friends that finally pushed me to publish this work.

First and foremost, my warmest thanks to my dear wife, Miriam nee Halberstadt, for her love and unending patience with me throughout the many years. I thank her deeply for reviewing the manuscript and offering her wise comments regarding both style and content. Miriam has anchored me to my family base providing stability and tranquility in my life, along with her appreciation of my travelling needs. She should continue to enjoy *nachas* from our expanded family in good health and joy.

At this time, I invoke the memory of my late father, ר' דוד ב"ר גרשון ז"ל, who brought me to my first Rav experience at the *Kinus Teshuva* before *Yom Kippur* of 1968. I recall my father sitting down with me on the previous Shabbat afternoon prepping me with the source material for the four-hour marathon *Shiur*. Looking back, I admit that I did not follow the entire *Shiur*. I did, however, pick up valuable bits and pieces of Torah information along the way. Nevertheless, I knew for sure from that moment on, that this man will become my Torah mentor!

I would like to thank my great Rebbe, *HaRav* Hershel Schachter שליט"א, for encouraging me time and again to publish this material for the benefit of all. His backing was a major contributing force in seeing this work to fruition. The preparation of this book afforded me the opportunity to cross-reference R' Schachter's three books on the Rav: *Nefesh HaRav, M'pnenei HaRav, and Divrei HaRav*.

I extend my deepest gratitude to R' Menachem Genack, R' Dovid Shapiro, and R' Prof. Carmi Horowitz who graciously reviewed the manuscript, along with offering their learned advice and thoughtful insights.

Dedicating this book to my older brother, R' Yosef Adler, is consistent with the Rav's character as a מכיר טוב – that of acknowledging genuine appreciation. My brother was a trailblazer for me in getting excited about the Rav in both capacities as Rabbi and educator. Without his invitation to me to serve as the Rav's driver, this book would never have happened, and I would never have become the person I am today. My brother, until this very day, serves as a constant source of accuracy in transmitting the Rav's opinions and thoughts. I pray that only good health should be his lot.

The publication of this book would not have transformed into reality were it not for the encouragement and assistance from long-standing friends, Bill and Rena Lewis (Chicago/Jerusalem). They should continue to be blessed with the best of health and much *nachas* from their expanded family.

I am deeply grateful to Tzvi Mauer and Pearl Friedman of Urim Publications for helping me translate a decades-old dream into a living reality. Their professional literary expertise, along with their patience and good-heartedness, has successfully guided me in reaping the fruits of my labors today.

ברוך . . . שהחיינו וקיימנו והגיענו לזמן הזה.

In a rare quote from the first Ashkenazi Chief Rabbi of *Eretz Yisrael, HaRav* Kook *zt"l*, the Rav cited the final words of every *Yom Kippur* prayer. "א-לוהי, עד שלא נוצרתי, איני כדאי. ועכשו שנוצרתי, כאילו לא נוצרתי" – "My Lord, before I was created, I was worthless, and now that I indeed have been created, it is as if I were not created." The understanding being: there's a reason why an individual is not born into a different era or generation, for he would have no purpose or mission to accomplish during that time. The problem, however, is that now that one does exist in his particular time, the feeling is that he has not, as yet, discovered his mission or purpose in life.[6]

I thank God for placing me precisely in this time and place having afforded me the opportunity of benefitting from this towering illustrious person, the Rav, who made Judaism

6. See the Rav's, *Out of the Whirlwind*, 2003, pp. 149–150, and A. Lustiger, *Derashot Harav*, 2003, pp. 50–51.

Preface

comprehensible to me and to so many others during our
lifetimes. In return, our modest efforts, in perpetuating these
seventy conversations, will only add to the Rav's posthumous
movement of lips forever. (See Sanhedrin 90b,כל מי שנאמרה הלכה
(בשמו בעולם הזה – שפתותיו דובבות בקבר

יהי זכרו של מו"ר הגרי"ד הלוי סולוביצ'יק ברוך לעד

Aaron Adler
Yerushalayim
Shevat, 5781

Hag HaSemikha, 1978 – Group Photo.
(*Private Collection*)

Hag HaSemikha,
1978
YU President, Rabbi
Dr. Norman Lamm
and the Rav (front
row, middle).
The brothers,
Rabbis Aaron and
Yosef Adler (second
row, middle).
(*Private Collection*)

I   Halakhic Decisions and Reasoning

The rabbi must know how to properly decide questions of Jewish law. "And they shall teach My people the difference between the holy and the common" (Ezekiel 44:23). This is the task of hora'ah, of providing Halakhic guidance.... To be expert in determining Halakha, one must not only be learned but he must also possess the intuition to understand the circumstances surrounding the Halakha and the context in which the question is asked.

— *The Rav*, ed. R' Aaron Rakefet-Rothkoff, Vol. 2, 1999, p. 59

What differentiates the approach of Rav Soloveitchik from that of Haredi poskim and makes him the authority figure of so-called "Modern Orthodoxy" is his endorsement of secular studies, including philosophy, his espousal of religious Zionism, and his pioneering of intensive Jewish education for women. Although these policies are not logically connected, they are closely related to each other, because they arise from the conviction that a Torat Hayyim addresses the realities of the world rather than seeks an escape from them. It is this religious philosophy, which engenders a unique approach to Halakha, which has made him into the posek par excellence of Modern Orthodoxy.

— R. Walter Wurzburger, "Rabbi Joseph B. Soloveitchik as *Posek* of Post-Modern Orthodoxy," *Exploring the Thought of Rabbi Joseph B. Soloveitchik*, ed. R' Marc Angel, 1977, pp. 5–6

Rendering Halakhic Decisions Appropriately

The Rav was of the opinion that the proper approach to rendering accurate Halakhic decisions must necessarily take into consideration not only the abstract theoretical issues at hand, but must also consider the subjective realities of the questioner. There were numerous cases where the Rav was asked by two individuals what seems to have been the identical question. Yet, each of them may have received different responses. This is due to the fact that the Rav was aware of the unique reality (economic, psychological, communal, etc...) of each of the questioners. Hence, the responses were appropriate to each one individually.

> This, by the way, is one of the reasons that the Rav did not publish Halakhic responsa during his lifetime, because no two situations are absolutely identical.

The following conversation vividly underscores this Halakhic approach:

תלמוד בבלי מסכת ברכות דף כח עמוד ב

משנה. רבי נחוניא בן הקנה היה מתפלל בכניסתו לבית המדרש וביציאתו תפלה קצרה. אמרו לו: מה מקום לתפלה זו? אמר להם: בכניסתי אני מתפלל שלא יארע דבר תקלה על ידי, וביציאתי אני נותן הודאה על חלקי.

גמרא. תנו רבנן: בכניסתו מהו אומר? יהי רצון מלפניך ה' א-להי שלא יארע דבר תקלה על ידי, ולא אכשל בדבר הלכה וישמחו בי חברי, ולא אומר על טמא טהור ולא על טהור טמא, ולא יכשלו חברי בדבר הלכה ואשמח בהם.

27

The Mishnah (Berachot 28b) reads:

> R' Nechunia b. HaKaneh used to say a prayer as he entered the Bet Midrash, and as he left – a short prayer....

The Talmud immediately supplies the text:

> "May it be Thy will, o Lord, my God, that no offence may occur through me, and that I may not err in a matter of Halakha, and that my colleagues may rejoice in me, and that I may not call impure – pure, or pure – impure"....

I questioned the Rav as to whether or not this "short prayer" was obligatory today for all Yeshiva students upon entering into the *Bet Midrash* each and every morning. The Rav responded that this prayer was never intended for students. Each individual is granted his or her individual intellectual capabilities. Either he has the capacity to comprehend the Talmud, the *Tosephot*, and the Rambam, or he doesn't. No call for Divine intervention will assist in unnaturally stretching the given human intellectual limits. However, continued the Rav, the prayer of *R' Nehunia b. HaKaneh* was deliberately designed for Halakhic decisors (פוסקים) who are entrusted and authorized to render Halakhic decisions. These decisions may, at times, impact deeply upon one's personal, financial, and psychological well being. One mustn't think that the Halakhic decision process is totally objective. Quite the contrary! Subjectivity is an extremely important ingredient in producing an "appropriate" decision. However, at times, the Halakhic decisor may not be privy to all available "hidden" pieces of information so critical for rending the "appropriate" decision. (Devarim 29:28, הַנִּסְתָּרֹת לַה' אֱ-לֹהֵינוּ) It is, therefore, most relevant to beseech of God a special Divinely-inspired guiding spirit (סייעתא דשמיא) prior to rendering Halakhic decisions. This is the essence of the "short prayer," "... that I may not err in a matter of impurity ... that I may not call impure – pure, or pure – impure." The colleagues (representing the questioners) will certainly "rejoice in me," not that they were thrilled by a novelty in resolving a contradiction in a Rambam text, but rather because of their full agreement and appreciation of the unique appropriateness of a decision applied to a very specific situation.

Aided by his effervescent Torah knowledge and experience, and guided by a keenly-developed Halakhic intuition, the Rav, at times, "knew" how to properly respond to a questioner prior to compiling all the relevant source material that would serve as the Halakhic basis for his decisions.[1]

Israel Schachter, son of R' Hershel Schachter, reports that his brother, R' Shay, (Young Israel of Woodmere), appeared as a guest on the "Behind the Bima" Podcast hosted by R' Efrem Goldberg of the Boca Raton Synagogue. Israel reported the following in a blog entitled, *A Giant of Halachik sensitivity – Corona & Ha'Rav Hershel Schachter*:

My brother set up a Zoom call for my father, R' Asher Weiss, and R' Mordechai Willig to discuss a very complex question that had come up. After hours of deliberation, my brother noticed that my father was being very quiet (though that it is not at all uncharacteristic for him) and seemed to be doing something else off to the side. When the call was over, my brother asked my father what he was distracted by towards the end of the call.

My father told him that he had been crying and reciting Tehillim (Psalms), praying for Divine assistance before making such a critical decision on behalf of the community.[2]

---

1. For a more comprehensive treatment on this pertinent Halakhic subject, see R' Aharon Lichtenstein, "The Human and Social Factors in Halakha," *Tradition*, Vol. 36, No.1, Spring 2002, pp. 1–25. In particular, note p. 7, the humble words of Rav Hayyim Volozhiner invoking Divine guidance in dealing with highly-sensitive "aguna" situations.

2. Extensive treatment of this subject can be found in R' Prof. Daniel Sperber, "The 'Friendly' Pesak," *The Importance of the Community Rabbi*, 2020, pp. 39–164.

For a sneak preview of this conversation, see R' Aharon Ziegler, *Halakhic Positions of the Rabbi Joseph B. Soloveitchik*, Vol. 4, 2007, pp. 3–4.

2   Strictness and Leniency in Cases of Doubt

Often, a *Posek* (Halakhic decisor) will not have a clear picture as to the proper direction of his decision. Dealing with a *safek* (doubt) situation is quite common in the rabbinic field. The *safek* can be in the Halakhic performance itself (e.g. a person cannot remember if he said a blessing over a *Mitzvah* act), or the *safek* lies in the various opinions on the subject. Rambam[3] adopts the Talmudic conclusion that in a *safek* involving a Biblical commandment, we are to render a strict decision. However, if the *safek* relates to a rabbinic issue, then we are to be lenient –
בשל תורה הלך אחר המחמיר, בשל סופרים הלך אחר המיקל.

Rambam continues to discuss in his next chapter[4] the Biblical prohibitions of adding (בל תוסיף) or deleting (בל תגרע) from any of the Halakhic details of any Law. He emphasizes the point that if we were to deliberately – or erroneously – present a matter of rabbinic Torah as Biblical, or vice versa, we would transgress one of these two above-mentioned sins.

In light of Rambam's opinion as stated, I questioned the Rav whether or not a *Posek* would be in violation of בל תוסיף if in a case of *safek* of a rabbinic nature, he were to take the stricter path? By ruling strictly on the subject – in a case of rabbinic *safek* – one is treating the matter as a Biblical concern. And, this is precisely the root of the בל תוסיף sin!

The Rav responded to me that this is the correct understanding

---

3. *Hilkhot Mamrim* 1:5, based upon *Avoda Zara* 7a.
4. Ibid., 2:1–9.

of the Rambam's words. Furthermore, on a private level, a person can be as strict as he wants to be – even in rabbinic *safek* situations. However, when formally teaching Torah or rendering Halahkic decisions, one ought to rule leniently on matters of *safek* in rabbinic issues. This is completely in line with the *Yerushalmi* comment (*Berakhot* 1:1) – אף על פי שאני מיקל לאחרים, מחמיר אני על עצמי.

3   Prenatal Testing

The Rav was once asked a question by someone whose wife was over forty years of age and pregnant. It was recommended to the woman to do prenatal genetic testing in order to rule out Tay Sachs disease or Down syndrome. The actual amniocentesis procedure runs a mild risk for miscarriage (0.25%–0.50%). More importantly, should any of these tests prove positive, the couple would then be faced with the dilemma of possibly aborting the affected fetus. The Rav strongly urged the couple not to go through with the amniocentesis procedure. He was less concerned with the marginal risk factor involved. His deep concern was what the consequences would be with the information if results were positive. In his opinion, an abortion designed to prevent the birth of a Down syndrome or Tay Sachs infant was unacceptable. His reasoning was that an abortion procedure performed not in the line of saving the mother's life would constitute a violation of "Thou shall not kill" (לא תרצח).[5] The Rav's assessment was that, for this couple, such was clearly not the case. His opinion was accepted by the couple without reservations.

In private conversation, the Rav confided in me that if, in fact, a couple would opt for an abortion of a positively-identified Tay Sachs fetus, one could possibly attempt to soothe the spiritual pain by reasoning that the psychological well-being of the mother may have played a major role in the decision to abort.

5. See R' Hershel Schachter, *Nefesh Harav*, 1994, p. 270.

The abortion per se could be viewed as a "life saver" for the desperate mother.

My brother, R' Yosef Adler, added that the Rav's above comment to me "shows the Rav's deep understanding of mental illness."

This last comment of the Rav deserves some elaboration, in light of the declared Halakhic opinion of the Rav who viewed abortions – in general – as a violation of "Thou shall not kill."[6]

Dr. Daniel Eisenberg in *Abortion in Jewish Law*, Science and Medicine, aish.com, writes:

Judaism recognizes psychiatric as well as physical factors in *evaluating the potential threat* that the fetus poses to the mother. However, the danger posed by the fetus (whether physical or emotional) must be both probable and substantial to justify abortion. The degree of mental illness that must be present to justify termination of a pregnancy has been widely debated by rabbinic scholars, without a clear consensus of opinion regarding the exact criteria for permitting abortion in such instances.[7] Nevertheless, all agree that were a pregnancy to cause a woman to become truly suicidal, there would be grounds for abortion.[8] However, several modern rabbinical experts ruled that since pregnancy-induced and post-partum depressions are treatable, abortion is not warranted.

An interesting postscript to this event is that over twenty years later, my wife and I hosted a young lady for a Shabbat who was studying that year at one of Jerusalem's Seminaries. She turned out to be the very healthy child born from the pregnancy described in this story!

6. I'm indebted to R' Menachem Genack for his learned comments regarding this point.

7. See Spero, Moshe, *Judaism and Psychology*, pp. 168–180.

8. Zilberstein, R' Yitzchak, *Emek Halakha, Assia*, Vol. 1, 1986, pp. 205–209.

4   Treating a Cerebral Death Patient

As a young Rabbi in 1977, serving at the Congregation Sons of Israel in Long Island City, NY, I dealt with a tragic situation of an automobile accident involving a couple from my community. The husband walked away from the accident with some minor scratches, while the wife was severely hurt. Lying in the hospital in a comatose state, the medical staff was quite pessimistic regarding her condition. After two weeks in intensive care, the family was informed that the EEG readings of the injured woman clearly showed that she was cerebrally brain dead. ("Cerebral death" is not to be confused with "brainstem death.") The prognosis for her recovery was infinitesimal at best. The family was given the option of preventing any active medical treatment in the event that pneumonia or other infectious conditions would develop. The woman would eventually die peacefully.

The family requested that I bring this Halakhic/moral dilemma to the Rav's attention. After paying careful attention to the details, the Rav reacted by saying that our Sages were not aware of "brain death," as understood today. The Rav invoked the Halakhic dictum: that an uncertainty in a Biblical issue, requires a strict ruling.[9] ספק דאורייתא – לחומרא. In spite of the neurological data provided, the woman was still Halakhically alive and should be treated for all future illnesses. The family gracefully accepted the Rav's opinion, and instructed the medical staff to continue all necessary medical treatment.

---

9. See R' Hershel Schachter, *Mipnenei HaRav*, 2001, p. 225.

In the course of three years, while in a comatose state, the family regularly visited the woman, updating her regarding relevant family news (an engagement of a daughter, the birth of a grandchild, etc.). Recordings were played to her, throughout these years, of family members talking to her and various musical selections.

During the interim three years, my family came on *Aliya* to Israel in 1979. (See Conversation #36 on the subject of my *Aliya*.) After over a year of separation from the family, I was told that in August, 1980, the woman had miraculously awakened from her coma and was able to communicate with her surroundings. A month had passed, and the woman was able to mouth out single words, and eventually put some words together. She informed her family that she absorbed all the information given to her during her comatose state! She was aware of the expansions having taken place in her family during this time. Several weeks later, in October, 1980, my family planned to visit the United States for a family wedding. I eagerly looked forward to visiting the woman in her rehab facility. But, as I descended from the plane in New York, I was informed that she had died earlier that day, and that we would be going directly to her funeral. The family had asked for me to eulogize her at the funeral. Immediately after the funeral, the husband requested of me to convey to the Rav his eternal gratitude for the Rav's decision of three years earlier – a decision which kept his wife alive. It was worth all the pain knowing that his wife was aware, all along, of the various additions to the family during those three years. The husband's request was, indeed, fulfilled in a matter of days.

5   Loss of Mucus Plug

Towards the end of a woman's pregnancy, almost signaling the onset of contractions, a woman may lose her mucus plug [a thick clump of cervical mucus that forms during pregnancy helping to protect the fetus]. There may be some light bleeding associated with the mucus plug loss. I posed the question to the Rav regarding the status of the woman in terms of ritual impurity in childbirth (טומאת לידה). The Rav responded that it's difficult to discern between the bleeding of the actual birth process and bleeding associated with a preliminary factor that can trigger the birth process. Hence, a strict opinion on this matter was in order – ספק דאורייתא לחומרא.

> My daughter, Rabbanit Dr. Chana Adler-Leserovits, (Gynecological Specialist, Northern Israel and Lecturer in modern Halakha at *Yeshivat Ma'aleh Gilbo'a*) referred me to Rav Elyashiv Knoll's *Ish V'isha*, (Hebrew), 2003, p. 205, where he unequivocally states that the mucus plug bleeding is considered uterine – and not cervical – bleeding. Hence, such an appearance would require our strict attention in rendering an appropriate Halakhic decision.

It is well known that the Rav sat down to a Thanksgiving Day turkey dinner in Boston in identification with this popular American holiday. Two obvious conclusions can be derived regarding the Rav's opinion on the Kashrut status of the American turkey, as well as his opinion that Thanksgiving Day is not, at all, a religious holiday, and hence, entails no prohibition of "following the ways of the Gentiles" (חוקת הגוי).[10]

Beyond these two important issues – their importance not withstanding – the Rav talked to me about the significance of exhibiting a patriotic spirit that went along with the festivities of Thanksgiving Day. American Jewry ought to show genuine appreciation to the country that, by and large, provided a safe haven for so many during distressful times throughout the world.

On the subject of not canceling his *Shiur* on Thanksgiving Day, the following anecdote comes to mind. The Rav usually flew from

---

10. See R' Hershel Schachter, *Nefesh HaRav*, 1994, p. 231. (The fowl referred to in HaRav Moshe Feinstein's *Iggrot Moshe* YD 1:34 citation appears to be the pheasant, and not the American turkey. Though somewhat related in species classification, they are categorically not identical). See also R' Aharon Ziegler, *Halakhic Positions of Rabbi Joseph B. Soloveitchik*, 1998, pp. 37–8. Note there (p. 38) the citation from Iggros Moshe, EH should read: 2:13. R' Ziegler writes: "Indeed, Rav Soloveitchik implied to his students that he and his family celebrated Thanksgiving, though he never canceled his *Shiur* that day."

Boston to New York City on Tuesday mornings, and returned to Boston on Thursday afternoon. During the year, there was never a need to reserve a seat on the Eastern Airlines NY-Boston shuttle flights. However, on the Thanksgiving Day weekend, the flights were overbooked with travelers and students from all over the country. The Rav would remind me to make a reservation for that late November Thursday flight back to Boston. While on the phone struggling to spell out the Rav's family name, he called out: "I fly as Mr. Joe Solo. It's less confusing!" When the Rav passed away on Pesah in 1993, my wife, Miriam, remarked: "He sure was a SOLO!"

7   Standing Up at a *Zimun* of Ten

There's a widespread custom of symbolically standing up momentarily during *Birkat Zimun* in the presence of a *Minyan* of ten (when נברך לא-לוהינו is said). Upon questioning the Rav regarding this custom, the Rav categorically said that this was not necessary.[11] The Rav explained that *Birkat Zimun* is linked directly to *Birkat HaMazon*. As the latter requires sitting in the place of eating, so, too, the former should be performed in a completely seated position.

> R' Menachem Genack explains in the Rav's words that the Lithuanian custom of not standing up at a *Zimun* of ten, is because *Zimun* is not to be associated with the category of "a matter of sanctity" (דבר שבקדושה) requiring ten, which would mitigate standing.[12] However, the custom in Poland was to stand momentarily while God's Name was being mentioned in the *Zimun* of ten. Apparently, the thinking there was that *Zimun* does conform to the category of "a matter of sanctity." (See Conversation #8.)

---

11. See R' Hershel Schachter, *Nefesh HaRav*, 1994, p. 148.
12. R' Menachem Genack, *Gan Shoshanim*, Vol. 1 (Hebrew), Chapter 7.

Responding to my question as to whether or not three women should be educated and/or encouraged to perform _Birkat Zimun_, the Rav cautioned that if the desire of the women came from a place of religious sincerity (יראת שמים), then the ruling should be affirmative. However, if the motivation stems from feminism, the ruling should be negative.

R' Aharon Ziegler[13] suggests that whereas the Rav's position on the upgraded _Zimun_ with ten (נברך לא-להינו) is not part of the Halakhic category of "a matter of sanctity" requiring a _Minyan_ (דבר שבקדושה), then it may be assumed that the Rav would allow ten women to constitute a quorum for the upgraded _Zimun_. I must, however, add that this assumption is mere speculation on R' Ziegler's part. As far as I know, the Rav never made such a claim.[14]

> R' Ziegler notes (p. 79) that the "_Mishneh Berurah_ was published in 1907" is partially accurate. Sections of the Hafetz Hayim's _Mishneh Berurah_ were already published in 1884, and already quoted by the R' Yechiel M. Epstein's _Arukh HaShulhan_ in the late 1880's. (See for example, _Arukh HaShulhan_, OH 11:22) The entire

---

13. Halakhic Positions of Rabbi Joseph B. Soloveitchik, Vol. 2, 2001, pp. 77–9.

14. For the Rav's Talmudic analysis of this subject, see _Reshimat Shiurim (Berakhot) of R' Yosef Dov Halevi Soloveitchik_, (ed. R' Zvi Reichman), 2012, pg. 490.

six volumes of *Mishneh Berurah* were, indeed, completed in 1907. The *Mishneh Berurah* comment, cited there by R' Ziegler, providing a rationale for the optional status of *Birkat Zimun* for women – "because women are not sufficiently proficient in reading these *Berachot*" – cannot be seriously considered in today's day and age of upgraded Jewish education for women. The Rav played a major role in this religious/social development. (See Conversation #34.)

9   Ten Women for *Megillah* Reading

Regarding the blessing recited at the conclusion of the *Megillah* reading, the *Rema* states (Shulhan Arukh, OH, 692:1) that it is only recited in the presence of a *Minyan* of ten. The *Rema* (ibid., 690:18) also raises the possibility that women may actually be counted towards the number ten vis-à-vis *Megillah* reading. To the Rav, this was not merely a "possibility," but a definite position. The reason is that the strong Halakhic recommendation to hear the *Megillah* with ten people is not to be associated with "a matter of sanctity" requiring a *Minyan* (דבר שבקדושה), but rather the concept of glorifying the Divine Name in the presence of multitudes (ברוב עם הדרת מלך). The Rav, therefore, instructed me to recite the final Blessing after *Megillah* reading for a group of ten (or more) women.[15]

> In a Halakhic Responsum to the Rabbinical Council of America regarding the possibility of imposed home quarantines during the 2020 Coronavirus pandemic, R' Hershel Schachter, citing the Rav and R' Moshe Feinstein, ruled that in such a crisis situation the *Megillah* could be heard via telephone

15. For a full discussion of the Halakhic nature of ten individuals for *Megillah* reading, see R' Menachem Genack, *Shiurei HaRav – Kri'at Shema and Tefillah*, 2010, pg. 232, note 100, analyzing the opposing viewpoints of the Hazon Ish and the Rav's uncle, R' Velvele Soloveitchik.

or video hookups. Yet, regarding the final blessing he wrote: "The *beracha* of *ha-rav es rivainu* however should not be made unless there is a *minyan* present where the *Megillah* is actually being read."[16]

16. A possible related discussion appears in R' Dovid Auerbach, *Halihot Beita*, 1983, pg. 113, note 13, regarding a woman reciting the *Gomel* thanksgiving blessing in the presence of ten women.

10   Repeating Two Verses in *Megillah* Reading

The Rav instructed me that during the *Megillah* reading on Purim, two verses with variant readings should be repeated. They are Esther 8:11 (להשמיד **להרוג** ולאבד/להשמיד **ולהרוג** ולאבד) and Esther 9:2 (ואיש לא עמד לפניהם/בפניהם). This was his practice in Boston.[17] The Rav's feelings were that each reading had its own understanding, and essentially they were both correct.[18]

> R' Mordechai Breuer z"l argues the point that we today can be definitive regarding the words, ולהרוג and לפניהם as being the original authentic words for these two verses. (See R' Mordechai Breuer, *Megadim* 10, 1990, מקראות שיש להם הכרע, pp. 97–106.)

---

17. See R' Mendi Gopin, *Davening with the Rav*, 2006, p. 121.
18. See R' Moshe Feinstein, *Iggrot Moshe*, OH 5:20.

11   Family Grave Visitations

It is generally known that in his early years, the Rav followed a long-standing family tradition (based upon the custom of the Vilna Gaon) to avoid grave visitations.[19] Questioning R' Schachter regarding the fact that after the Rav's wife passed away in 1967, the Rav would visit her grave every Friday (!), R' Schachter commented to me that apparently, at that time, the Rav changed his behavior on this matter. Apparently so, for on his father's *Yahrzeit* (3 Shevat) in 1975, the Rav asked me to take him to a Brooklyn, NY cemetery to visit the gravesite of his father, R' Moshe Soloveitchik *zt"l*.

At the cemetery, standing in the Chevra Anshei Brisk plot near his father's gravesite, the Rav quite unemotionally – in the Lithuanian tradition – simply recited a chapter of the Psalms. I got a firsthand glimpse into a *Brisker Azkara* – dry, sterile, no tears, etc.... And, then, suddenly, an about-face occurred! The Rav took my hand and – like a grandfather – warmly guided me through the myriad of monuments in that plot. He paused at several of the monuments while nostalgically reflecting upon some of those departed whom he obviously knew well. He was smiling all the way through and was clearly in high spirits. "This individual," the Rav would say, "was a serious תלמיד חכם (scholar)". Another person was described as a more fun-loving individual (a "kibbetzer," in the Rav's words!). The world requires all types of people, remarked the Rav. During this visit,

19. See R' Hershel Schachter, *Nefesh HaRav*, 1994, p. 254.

the Rav silently revealed to me the duality within his complex personality.

> Regarding the Rav's lack of adherence to family tradition, there have been other occasions where the Rav deviated – for good reason – from certain family customs. He would generally explain his practice to his students in the context of a Shiur. Escorting the Rav, as I did that afternoon, in the cemetery, the Rav's silence on this matter was deafening. I never got the impression that the Rav was engaged in an activity that went against the grain of his family tradition.

Tevilat Keilim for Electrical Appliances

The Halakha of ritual immersion in a *Mikveh* of metallic or glass vessels acquired from non-Jews (טבילת כלים) becomes complicated when the electrical apparatus of an appliance is an integral part of the vessel. Some have suggested that the entire vessel – along with its electrical components – be fully immersed, and then placed to dry out. The downside of this suggestion is that, in all likelihood, the vessel would be permanently ruined or short circuited. An alternative recommendation that only the metallic or glass portions of the vessels be immersed while leaving the electrical areas out of the *Mikveh* was considered by the Rav as unacceptable, because – by definition – ritual immersion (for both humans and vessels) must necessarily be absolute and not partial. The only practical suggestion the Rav could offer was to disavow ownership (הפקר) from the vessel by a declaration in the presence of three people, and then by leaving it outdoors in public for several minutes while unattended. One should then re-acquire the vessel from the state of non-ownership and would, thereby, be exempt from the Halakhic obligation for ritual immersion.

> During the 2020 worldwide coronavirus pandemic, the *Mikveh* for vessels was closed in most Jewish communities. The above-stated solution of disavowing ownership in the presence of three people was adopted by R' Hershel Schachter, who added that the three individuals could be "present" over the telephone or internet lines.

Replacing Vacuum Cleaner Bags before Pesah

There are Pesah preparation manuals that include the replacing of vacuum cleaner bags before Pesah because, in all likelihood, the machine picked up some *Hametz* during the course of the past year. These bags are disposable bags with no possibility of opening and shaking them out. The Rav, however, suggested three reasons why this annual replacement was not necessary. First of all, the *Hametz* particles that may have been sucked into the vacuum cleaner bag are totally inaccessible. The rule (Mishnah, *Pesahim* 2:3) that *Hametz* caught under a collapsed wall חמץ שנפלה עליו מפולת הרי הוא כמבוער applies to this situation, and, hence, no prohibition exists for this inaccessible *Hametz* to remain in one's possession during Pesah. Furthermore, whatever *Hametz* that may have been picked up from the floor will usually be ground into crumbs by the time it enters the vacuum cleaner bag. We can then invoke the Talmudic dictum (*Pesahim* 6b) that crumbs are insignificant (פירורין הא לא חשיבי), and, therefore, employing both rationales, there would be no violation of possessing H*ametz* in one's domain on Pesah (בל יראה בל ימצא).

Additionally, the Rav suggested, we could augment the aforementioned Halakhic logic by relying, in this case, upon the view that one could disavow ownership over any **known** *Hametz* (ביטול חמץ **ידוע**) in the vacuum cleaner bag. The Rav's words reflect the view of R' Mano'ah (commentary to Rambam, Hilkhot Hametz U'Matzah, 2:1–2:

"והביעור מועיל בחמץ הידוע לו ואינו יכול לבערו, כגון נפלה עליו מפולת."[20]

---

20. Two opposing views, based upon variant textual readings of Rambam's *Hilkhot Hametz U'Matzah* 2:2, are discussed in Rambam's *Sefer HaMitzvot*, Positive Commandment 156 (editor, R' Yosef Kafiah), pg. 139, note 75. For a detailed Halakhic analysis of these variant readings, see the commentary, Mar'eh HaPanim, to Yerushalmi Pesahim 4a. See also Aaron Adler, "The Relationship of Rambam to the Yerushalmi" (Hebrew), in the *R' Yosef Kafiah Memorial Volume*, 2001, pg. 208, note 30, and pp. 230–235.

14   Purchasing *Hametz* Products after Pesah

Our Sages introduced a rabbinic restriction forbidding benefit from Jewish-owned *Hametz* not dealt with properly before Pesah (e.g. disavowing ownership, selling to a Gentile, etc.). In practical terms, a Jewish-owned food establishment or supermarket where *Hametz* was not sold to a Gentile would be off limits for some time after Pesah until it can reasonably be assumed that post-Pesah fresh stock has entered into the store and filled the shelves. Many years ago, people spoke of a six-week waiting period. Later, this number had already been reduced to thirty days. In spite of the fact that modern day supermarket chains have rapid turnover rates, nevertheless, the current OU website recommends twenty five days to be on the safe side.[21]

In discussing the issue with the Rav, his opinion was that given the modern-day mass production techniques in the food industry, one could be comfortable by simply waiting just one week (!) after Pesah, in order to shop in such establishments.

> In conversation with R' Menachem Genack, CEO of OU Kosher, I was informed that regarding many of the US supermarket outlets, the one-week waiting period after Pesah was, indeed,

21. See HaRav Moshe Feinstein, *Iggrot Moshe*, OH 4:96 for a full discussion on the matter. His inclination is to estimate a 50% chance that there is fresh merchandise on the shelves. At that point, one could freely purchase in such a store.

adequate. However, there is a complicating factor involved when the distributors of *Hametz* food products are also non-observant Jews. This could significantly increase the waiting period after Pesah – which is the root of the OU recommendation to wait twenty-five days!

15   Shabbat Candles in Homes of Others

As a young newly-wed in 1975, I asked the Rav, on behalf of my wife, Miriam, where Shabbat candles should be lit when we were guests in the homes of our parents. Could she light the candles in the vicinity of our mother's candles, or would it be necessary to choose a different location (perhaps even a different room in the apartment) to light her candles. At first, the Rav reacted that there's something to be said about having my wife light in a slightly different location. The reason is that if Shabbat candles were already lit in a particular location, then the desired illumination of that area has already been accomplished by those Shabbat candles. However, on second thought, he quickly reversed his opinion and said that every additional burning candle illuminates the area in a greater way. And, one may recite the blessing and light candles for any additional illumination of that area.[22]

---

22. See R' Aharon Ziegler, *Halakhic Positions of Rabbi Joseph B. Soloveitchik*, Vol. I, 1998, pp. 3–4. There, the Rav was obviously reflecting his earlier thinking on the subject.

16 Hanukah Candles in Modern Times

The ideal time to light Hanukah candles is subject to differences of opinions in the Halakhic world. Most Jews, including those residing in Israel, abide by the opinion found in *Shulhan Arukh* OH 672:1, stating that lighting is to commence at the appearance of stars (צאת הכוכבים). While others (custom of Gaon of Vilna, based on Rambam's view) begin the lighting immediately after sundown. All this is based upon how one interprets the Talmudic line (Shabbat 21b): מצותה משתשקע החמה עד שתכלה רגל מן השוק. The Rav followed his family tradition of lighting at sundown as per the Vilna Gaon (which is the current practice of many Jerusalem residents).

The question is how long do the candles have to burn? In the above-quoted Talmudic line, the answer is until the people leave the marketplace (meaning, until no soul is to be seen outdoors any longer that evening). In Rambam's twelfth century environment, this was translated into approximately half an hour after sunset. This half-hour time framework became commonplace throughout Europe even when lighting indoors and at a later hour.

The Rav, however, believed that we still should follow that original idea, and have the candles burn until the hour that people have returned home from work. In New York City, the rush hour traffic in the evening is from 5:00pm until 7:00pm. The Rav (who used wax candles and not oil due to dexterity issues) would use thick Shabbat candles for his Hanukah candles each

53

night melted on aluminum foil.[23] He believed that in modern days, the half-hour time frame lost its original relevance. In the Rav's opinion, the Hanukah candles should burn for at least two full hours after sundown.[24]

23. See R' Hershel Schachter, *Nefesh HaRav*, 1994, pg. 226.

24. See R' Aharon Ziegler, *Halakhic Positions of Rabbi Joseph B. Soloveitchik*, Vol. III, pp. 110–111 for a different understanding of the Rav's position.

17

Torah Reading Outside the Framework of Prayer

A Halakhic discussion exists regarding allowance of a formal Torah reading outside the framework of Prayer. The Rav concurred with those who held that it was permissible to read a scheduled Torah reading later on during the day. (See *Mishnah Berurah*, 135:1) However, the Rav believed that this later reading must necessarily be in the presence of at least ten adult males who have not, as yet, heard the Torah reading that morning.

Although the Rav regularly flew in from Boston on Tuesday mornings, there was a particular urgency on one Monday morning for the Rav to arrive a day earlier than usual. The Rav was pressed for time leaving Boston that Monday, and did not hear the Torah reading that morning. Upon arrival in New York, he asked me if I could search the campus of YU and locate another nine students who have not, as yet, heard that morning's Torah reading. I assured the Rav that it wouldn't be a problem rounding up nine such YU students! Indeed, it didn't take long to organize the *Minyan* for the Rav's Torah reading (and their's as well!). But I did notice that for some of these students, it would be their first encounter with the Rav in such a close situation.[25]

25. See R' Hershel Schachter, *Divrei HaRav*, 2010, pg. 152, in the name of R' Menachem Genack, on the question of *Kaddish* recitation after such a Torah reading. See also R' Menachem Genack, *Shiurei HaRav – Kri'at Shema and Tefillah*, 2010, pg. 231–232, on the Rav's reporting the differences of opinion between his two grandfathers – R' Hayim Soloveitchik of Brisk and R' Elya Feinstein of Pruzhan – over whether Torah reading is an individual obligation (חובת היחיד) or a communal obligation (חובת הציבור).

18   "Glatt Kosher Meat"

Until 1956, local rabbinical authorities in the United States certified whether or not commercially-produced meat and meat products were Kosher. With the wave of Hungarian ultra-Orthodox migrants that year, a new upgraded standard for Kosher meat had been introduced – "Glatt Kosher." The word, *glatt*, is Yiddish, and its meaning is "smooth." After the initial slaughtering of a kosher animal, a determination had to be made if the animal was healthy enough to live another twelve months. If the animal had sustained an internal injury that would cause it to die within a year, the animal was ruled unfit for Jewish consumption (*Treife*). The most sensitive of the internal organs were the animal's lungs. Many animal lungs were seen to be perforated with scar tissue having grown on the lung's outer membrane. If this were to occur, then the initial examination of the lung for smoothness would fail. The lung would have to be tested for air bubbles in a tub of water. No visible air bubbles means kosher. Otherwise, the animal is ruled to be not kosher. "Glatt" means that the animal passed its initial inspection with no adhesions to the membrane at all. Many of the Hungarian Jews would only consume meat when no Halakhic questions were generated around the animal.

With time, the concept of Glatt Kosher became so popular in the United States that hardly anybody would eat "regular" Kosher meat. The Rav told me, in 1976, that the pressure to market Glatt Kosher meat was so great, that the supervisors were passing off as "Glatt" even if one, or two, or even three adhesions had to be examined!

The Rav then explained that there is Halakhic proof that "Glatt" is not the basic standard of *Kashrut*. There is a Halakhic norm referred to as רוב בהמות כשרות (the majority of animals are kosher). That is to say that had we slaughtered every kosher animal in the world, the majority would pass inspection as being certified Kosher. (This is the reason that we're permitted to drink milk and consume milk products.) The Rav told me that in the 1930s and 1940s when he was communally involved in the kosher status of meat in the Boston area, he kept careful records of the slaughtering results. He said that 21% of all Kosher-slaughtered animals were ultimately ruled non-kosher. The age-old tradition of רוב בהמות כשרות was clearly upheld. However, while the majority of the animals might ultimately become kosher meat, the majority were not "Glatt!" Hence, the requirement for Glatt Kosher meat was a stringent view (חומרא), and did not reflect the basic Halakhic standard.

19   *Gomel* **Blessing for Air Travel**

The Talmud (Berakhot 54b) teaches the Halakha of the four individuals who are required to offer the blessing of thanksgiving. They include the sea traveler, the desert crosser, the healed, and the released from prison. יורדי הים, הולכי מדברות, ומי שהיה חולה ונתרפא, ומי שהיה חבוש בבית האסורים. The practical application of this Halakha is the recitation of the *Gomel* blessing in the presence of ten adults.

Modern day air travel has generated the question as to whether or not this *Gomel* blessing must be recited after a routine landing on the ground. R' Moshe Feinstein[26] says that there's no fundamental difference between air travel and travel over the high seas. Therefore, in his opinion, one ought to recite the *Gomel* after each flight. R' Eliezer Waldenberg[27] makes the distinction between domestic flights and overseas flights. In a pre-9/11 responsum, R' Waldenberg claims that the dangers in air travel have to do with hijackings. These don't take place on domestic flights. Today, we tragically know differently.

The Rav believed that the four illustrations listed in the aforementioned Talmudic source all speak of life-threatening scenarios. Modern day air travel is, statistically, four thousand times safer than riding a car! Therefore, if all goes well with the

---

26. Iggrot Moshe OH 2:59.
27. Tzitz Eliezer 11:14.

flight, and nobody was in any mortal danger, there would be no need for a *Gomel* blessing.[28]

> See R' Jekutiel Judah Halberstam's *Divrei Yatziv*, OH, (87), which discusses the *Gomel* recitation requirement while on the ground awaiting a connection flight! It seems reasonable that commercial pilots and flight attendants flying multiple flights daily would not be required, after each leg, to recite *Gomel*. My son, Eitan – an El Al commercial pilot – asserts that the Rav's opinion is the most appropriate for himself and his colleagues.

28. See R' Hershel Schachter, *Mipnenei HaRav*, 2001, pg. 60.

20   No "Amen" Response after *Gomel* Blessing

The Shulhan Arukh[29] teaches that the *Gomel* blessing elicits a direct response from those assembled, מי שגמלך כל טוב הוא יגמלך כל טוב סלה. The question is whether or not the standard response of "Amen" is also required after hearing the entire blessing? Many Halakhists seem to indicate that there is a need for the "Amen" response.[30] The Rav, however, believed that the response of מי "שגמלך" " supplants the requirement of an "Amen" response immediately after hearing the blessing.

29. OH 219:2.
30. See Arukh HaShulhan, OH 219:5.

The Rav delivering the historic *Shiur* at Stern College – 1977.
(*Photo: Yeshiva University Archives, Public Relations Photo Collection*)

The Rav delivering a *Shiur* at
YU – 1960s.
*(Photo: Yeshiva University
Archives, Public Relations Photo
Collection)*

Rav Soloveitchik's greatest impact was as teacher of Talmud (in Hebrew, a rebbe or rosh yeshiva) at Yeshiva University, where he taught from 1941 until 1985.... The Rav's Talmud Shiur was not only the focal point of all his activities – it was the prism through which he viewed everything else. He frequently defined himself as "a melamed," a teacher, noting that this is also a description of God ("ha-melamed Torah le-ammo Yisrael").

— R' Reuven Ziegler, Majesty and Humilty, 2012, p. 34

It is here in America that I first started to properly appreciate Jewish education. This morning, on my porch, I heard Jewish children speaking about the bacon and eggs they had for breakfast. When I come into a day school and see Jewish children reciting the Shema and making blessings before they eat, I truly value Torah education. It is the contrast which makes it so worthwhile!

— The Rav, ed. R' Aaron Rakefet-Rothkoff, Vol. 2, 1999, pp. 14–15

21 | On Being Referred to as "The Rav"

As mentioned in the Preface, HaRav Soloveitchik was known by his students and followers simply as "The Rav." An interesting tidbit regarding this compact, but respectful, title, "The Rav," is related by R' Hershel Schachter in the name of R' Menachem Genack,[1] noting that the Rav once quipped how interesting it is that R' Moshe Feinstein (the Rav's cousin once removed) was referred to as "The *Rosh Yeshiva*," in spite of the fact that his popularity surrounded his Halakhic decision-making abilities as a Rav. By contrast, he was called "The Rav" in spite of the fact that his principle calling was to the teaching of Torah – more of a *Rosh Yeshiva* type.

I, myself, can testify participating in the Rav's *Shiur* at the time, when the daily attendance list registered one hundred students. However, the double classroom on the fourth floor of Yeshiva University's Furst Hall held one hundred and twenty students at any given *Shiur*. The additional twenty were unofficial "guests" from other New York *yeshivot* who came regularly to audit the Rav's *Shiur*. It was common practice, in Lithuanian yeshiva circles, to address a *Rosh Yeshiva* in third person – as an act of reverence – by saying: "the *Rosh Yeshiva* said...." As it was, one of these visitors interrupted the Rav with a question, beginning with: "The *Rosh Yeshiva* said...." Before allowing him to continue, the Rav exploded by exclaiming: "I am NOT the *Rosh*

1. *Divrei HaRav*, 2010, p. 207.

67

Yeshiva here! Dr. Belkin, on the fifth floor, is the *Rosh Yeshiva*! I am a *'melamed'* – a *'poshete* [simple] *melamed.'* Ich bin a gutte [I am a good one (!)], but [nevertheless] a *'melamed.'*" "Okay," continued the Rav, "now what is your question?"

22 ___ Down to Earth Rabbis and Educators

In discussing with the Rav my own future prospects of getting involved in the rabbinate and in education, he pointed out that Rabbis and teachers of Torah are to be compared to the angels (i.e. spiritual messengers of God). The topic of angels is raised by Rambam in *Hilkhot Yesodei HaTorah* 2:7. There, Rambam posits that the angels are assigned ten different names, for each name represents another rung on the spiritual ladder in descending order. The most connected to the upper heavenly spheres are the "holy animals" (חיות הקודש), while the lowest order are known as "humanoid" (אישים). It is precisely this lower order of angels who make contact with human beings in the Bible. While still assuming their spiritual angelic identity, they also have "their two feet on the ground." The Rav said that our generation needs more Rabbis and educators who, simultaneously, radiate spiritual teachings along with this-worldly mannerisms. This includes an awareness of social events and cultural appreciation. Today, the אישים type will be much more successful over his חיות הקודש counterpart. In retrospect, these were sage words indeed!

23   Versatility in Teaching

Teaching is an art form. Art requires talent. And, talent demands cultivation and training. The Rav was a strong believer in teachers talented enough to successfully shift gears from one level of audience to another. In the area of versatility, the Rav was a pro. He could teach advanced Talmud students, laymen with limited Torah knowledge, the young and the old, in mixed settings of both men and women. He once remarked to me that he would cherish going into a first-grade class and teaching the children *Humash* and *Rashi*! He continued by saying that this wouldn't be easy for him. The challenge would include knowing the language level of the children, awareness of their limited comprehension and attention span, along with delivering the message effectively even for the tender young students. He would have to work hard properly preparing such a class. But, he was ready to accept the mandate if offered. The Rav added that the phrase found in Synagogues, "Know whom you are Facing" (דע לפני מי אתה עומד), referring to the individual praying before God, is no less relevant for the teacher standing before his/her audience. "Know thy crowd," said the Rav to me. Don't overshoot, for you will lose them, and certainly don't undershoot, for this would be insulting to their intelligence. Adjust your levels carefully and appropriately in all teaching commitments.

24   Ingredients for a Good Shiur

I once asked the Rav if he could suggest a list of ingredients that go into "cooking up" a good *Shiur*. He immediately responded: 70% matter and 30% entertainment! The truth is that the Rav possessed a keen sense of humor, and intuitively knew how to use it successfully during the course of a *Shiur*. Properly timed, this dose of humor would relax the otherwise tense atmosphere prevailing during the *Shiur*. These brief distractions from the seriousness of the topic at hand only amplified the exhilaration of grasping the novellae emanating from the *Shiur* itself.

> An example of the Rav employing his dramatic flare and humor took place on the first day of *Shiur* in September of 1975. The Rav, who unilaterally decided each year which tractate of Talmud would be studied, came in and began taking a student poll as to what should be studied that year. Many different tractates were suggested by a variety of students. After hearing everyone's suggestion, the Rav went right on to announce what he had in mind all along – not matching any of the students' suggestions! Looking up at the class, he says: Are you wondering why I even asked you? Because I'm a democrat! However, משה עולה על גביהן, as Moses had overriding veto power over the seventy-man *Sanhedrin*, so, too, does he enjoy this veto power in place of Moses!

When asked how much time he spent preparing a good *Shiur* (Of course, every *Shiur* the Rav delivered was a "good *Shiur*"), the Rav responded after a moment's thought, "seventy two years!" The Rav was seventy-two years old at the time (1975). He clarified that somehow the sum-total of one's learning and life's experiences should be reflected in every *Shiur*!

> I actually contemplated buying the Rav a birthday gift that year. I had in mind a tie clip with an engraving lifted out of *Mishnah Yada'im* 3:5, "מקובל אני מפי ע״ב זקן." For many, including myself, the Rav represented the link of the unbroken tradition (מסורה) to our glorious past. The Rav connected us to his grandfather, R' Hayim, to the Vilna Gaon, to the Rambam, and the members of the Sanhedrin of two millenia ago, representing the ע״ב זקן.

On one occasion, escorting the Rav back to his apartment after a four-hour marathon *Yahrzeit Shiur* – a *Shiur* packed with sensational novellae interpreting difficult Rambam texts – I asked the Rav if he really believed that Rambam had all these great ideas in mind while writing his book. The Rav looked at me and said: "What's the difference, was it not a good *Shiur*!" I was somewhat stunned by the answer. The next morning, in conversing with the Rav's son, R' Prof. Haym Soloveitchik, he told me that it was perfectly legitimate to use a text (Halakhic or otherwise – as in the United States Constitution) to launch ideas. Irrespective whether or not Rambam entertained those ideas, the very ideas themselves must be considered authentic Torah and treated as such.

25   Elevating the Mediocre Students

The Rav was blessed with exceptionally gifted students. While thousands of students and followers viewed the Rav as their "principal teacher" (רב מובהק), the Rav himself would naturally have a select few "principal students" (תלמידים מובהקים).

> In my humble opinion, the number one תלמיד מובהק was the Rav's son-in-law, my Rebbe, HaRav Aharon Lichtenstein zt"l – a towering Torah personality in his own right who lived and breathed the Rav day in and day out.

Regarding the רב מובהק status, Rambam (*Hilkhot Talmud Torah* 5:9) defines this category as the individual who taught a student the bulk of his student's wisdom (שלמד ממנו רוב חכמתו). The Rav understood the phrase, רוב חכמתו, not quantitatively, but rather the teacher who defined the student's religious personality.

Although he was a teacher who demanded and strove for excellence, he was not remiss in his responsibilities as a teacher towards the mediocre students as well. The newly-defined רב מובהק status could now be linked to the multitude of students and followers who viewed the Rav as theirs.

What fascinated the less than excellent students about the Rav? If such students had difficulty keeping up with the pace of the *Shiur*, why bother regularly attending such *Shiurim*? The Rav, himself, provided the answer. Rambam teaches that one should pay a visit to ones רב מובהק on the three pilgrimage festivals (חייב אדם להקביל פני רבו ברגל).

The Rav explained that this Halakha relates to the tri-annual Biblical command to rendezvous with God at His resting place – the Temple in Jerusalem. In the post-Temple era, this rendezvous takes place symbolically at the home of the רב מובהק, temporarily substituting for the Temple in re-enacting this experience.

> There's a Yiddish song which poetically describes one's "ascent" to R' Menachem Mendel of Kotsk as parallel to ascending the Temple Mount during the pilgrimage festivals:
>
> קיין קאצק פארט מען נישט,
> קיין קאצט גייט מען.
> ווייל קאצט איז דאך במקום המקדש,
> קיין קאצט דארף מען עולה-רגל זיין

Our Sages teach us (Yerushalmi, Sukkah 5:1) that Jonah, the Prophet, regularly frequented the Temple on the pilgrimage festivals, and was inspired by a Divine spirit as he attended the rejoicing at the place of the water-drawing (יונה בן אמיתי מעולי רגלים היה ונכנס לשמחת בית השואבה ושרת עליו רוח הקודש). Given his natural abilities, Jonah was apparently not up to becoming a prophet. However, he was swept up and elevated into prophecy as a direct result of this Divine rendezvous at the Temple. On the level of substituting for the Temple of old, the Rav also allowed for mediocre students to grow beyond their natural capabilities by creating the atmosphere of such Divine rendezvous. Hence, many students and followers were elevated and uplifted to unimagined spiritual heights. This was an educational desideratum for the Rav.

> The Rav's active engagement with the less-than-elite audiences (mediocre students, laymen, and youth) was highlighted in the towering eulogy penned by the Rav's son-in-law, R' Prof Yizhak Twersky zt"l, in *K'Ma'ayan HaMitgaber*, (Hebrew), ed. R' Prof. Carmi Horowitz, 2020, pp. 678–681.

26   Educating Towards *Aliya* to Israel

In discussing the subject of educating the youth and the adult population regarding the significance of making *Aliya* to Israel, the Rav was very emphatic that the absolutely wrong tactic would be to scare the people into believing that another Holocaust, God forbid, was on its way. He did not believe that this was the case, nor did he think that such a method was educationally sound. The Rav advocated the positive. He advised me to inculcate in people the sensitivity towards the Sanctity of the Land, the agricultural commandments of Eretz Yisrael, and to deal with the Halakhic issue of *Yishuv Eretz Yisrael* (settlement of the Land of Israel).

The Rav also felt that on a practical level, if one's *Aliya* to Israel was based exclusively upon Torah values, this would help overcome some of the day to day hardships involved in the absorption process in an unfamiliar country.

27   Educating the Non-Religious Students

Throughout North America, only 10% of Jewish children receive any kind of Jewish education on the elementary school level. While on the high school level, the numbers dip to 1%. It is, therefore, no accident that assimilation and intermarriage rates have climbed above the 50% mark. With these statistics in mind, many in the YU circle have dedicated their lives to קירוב רחוקים (bringing the alienated Jews closer). This is expressed by involvement in youth organization activities and formal teaching in the various afternoon supplementary Hebrew school programs.

The Rav believed that we should accept teaching positions in Synagogue-affiliated schools – even if the Synagogue itself does not meet up to Halakhic standards. I, personally, was involved in such a school, affiliated with the Conservative Movement's East Meadow Jewish Center in Long Island, NY. This Synagogue was defined as a "right wing" Conservative Synagogue, with YU-trained R' Israel Noble *z"l* at its helm, and R' Aharon Ziegler (author of *Halakhic Positions of Rabbi Joseph B. Soloveitchik*) as its school principal. We were able to introduce the Orthodox Union's youth organization, NCSY, into the system alongside the USY Conservative counterpart.

At East Meadow, as well as in other similar Synagogues, there was a weekly Junior Congregation for the youngsters to attend on Shabbat. The problem we faced was that we were certain that the children would be driven by their parents to the Synagogue on Shabbat. Could we, as teachers, encourage our young students to attend the Junior Congregation services when, in fact, we would be accomplices to the desecration of Shabbat?

R' Schachter reports that the Rav explicitly forbade Rabbis from inviting adult congregants to their Shabbat meals, if their mode of transportation would mean coming by car.[2]

However, the issue presented to the Rav dealt with the education of children. To R' Moshe Feinstein, there was no difference between children and adults.[3] However, the Rav saw this differently. He asked me what I was out to accomplish – to teach Shabbat or Prayer. I told him that I wanted the students to feel comfortable in a Synagogue setting. My long-range goal was to encourage the children to favor the NCSY group over the USY. At the NCSY Shabbaton programs, much time is spent in the Synagogues. The strategy was that in the NCSY atmosphere, the children would learn to adopt more and more *Mitzvot*. The Rav said that unlike the conversion process, in which the potential convert must accept all or nothing, in cases of קירוב רחוקים one should take one *Mitzvah* at a time. If my educational goal was to foster proper prayer habits, then Shabbat would have to wait for a brighter day. The Rav homiletically interpreted the verse in Shemot 29:37, כָּל הַנֹּגֵעַ בַּמִּזְבֵּחַ יִקְדָּשׁ , as meaning that our job as educators is to get the students to come in contact with something holy. The persuasive power of Torah will then take over. (To a large degree the קירוב work performed by the emissaries of the Lubavitcher Rebbe *zt"l* function in a similar way.)

The Rav also felt that we could educate these children by having them recite the appropriate blessings over food, in spite of the fact that the food may not be kosher.

---

2. See R' Hershel Schachter, *Divrei HaRav*, 2010, p. 270. Similarly, R' Moshe Feinstein maintained the identical opinion. See Iggrot Moshe, OH 1:99.

3. See Iggrot Moshe, 1:98.

> The rule of thumb is that one should not make a blessing over
> non-kosher food. This is based upon Psalms 10:3, ה אֵץ נָאֵץ בֵּרֵךְ וּבֹצֵעַ'.
> If eating in a life-threatening situation, some are of the opinion
> that one should recite the blessings over the non-kosher food.

Although the Rav never mentioned this to me specifically, it is
possible that his line of thinking had something to do with a
positive attitude on the question of פיקוח נפש בסכנה רוחנית (the
allowance to override Torah violations in face of spiritually
danger situations).[4]

---

4. See R' Shaul Yisraeli, Tehumin (2), 1981, pp. 27–34, and the *Eretz
Hemdah* Responsa, *B'mar'ot HaBazak* (3), 2015.

28   Unpublished Books

In the Soloveitchik family tradition, the Rav was reluctant to publish full-length books in his lifetime. (See Conversation #69.) It is, nevertheless, interesting to note that the Rav had plans to publish several most interesting works in different areas of Torah.

It was not unusual in his public discourses for the Rav to quote, and develop an idea, from the Tanya (primary work of the Habad movement, authored by its founder, R' Shneur Zalman of Liadi). The Rav made mention privately that there was, in preparation, a running commentary of the entire Tanya! The Rav, apparently, was so satisfied with his understanding of the Tanya that he once quipped: "one day we'll see who understood the Tanya better – me or the Rebbe!"

Another book idea in gestation was a full-length commentary to the first half of the Book of Bamidbar. There, the Rav pointed out a recurring use by our Sages, of connecting each of the Biblical sections (למה נסמכה). This unusual phenomenon, according to the Rav, would indicate a possible common thread running from *Parshat Naso* through *Parshat Korah*. Unfortunately, such a book was never published. However, bits and pieces did appear in article form, throughout the years, that touched on the "connection" theme between the various Torah sections.[5]

Yet another book – possibly completed, but unpublished –

---

5. See the Rav's *Divrei Hashkafa*, 1992, pp. 57–69, and *HaAdam V'Olamo*, pp. 163–176.

was an in-depth analysis of the use of electricity on Shabbat. From the turn of the twentieth century, this issue has been subject to serious Halakhic scrutiny.[6] The Rav felt that he had a major contribution to offer on the subject based upon his comprehension of the physics of electricity. In all likelihood, the practical net results would have been a more lenient Halakhic opinion regarding the use of electricity on Shabbat.

> Among the Bostonians, it is well known that the Rav approved the use of turning on – not turning off – electric lights on *Yom Tov*. This opinion was apparently shared by R' Yekhiel M. Epstein *zt"l*, author of *Arukh HaShulhan*, in his preserved responsum found in R' Yehuda Leib HaKohen Maimon's *Sarei HaMei'ah*, 1956 (6), pp. 115–116. (I salute R' Dovid Shapiro for providing me with this source.)

6. Summarizing all the various opinions on this subject, see the Talmudic Encyclopedia, Vol. 18, (Ed. R' Shlomo Yosef Zevin), pp. 155–190, and Appendix, pp. 641–782.

                         Perseverant to Understand

The Rav, in his pursuit of excellence, was quite perseverant when it came to unresolved Halakhic or textual queries. He would invest much time and intellectual energy contemplating an issue until it would finally be resolved to his satisfaction.

On one occasion, towards the end of a three-hour *Shiur* at YU, the Rav raised a question regarding the exact meaning of a phrase in *Rashi*. He began thinking aloud exploring various possibilities. After fifteen minutes, he lowered his head in deep meditation. The Rav kept this up for almost forty-five minutes! The silence in the room was deafening. Several of the students had to leave the room in order to get to their afternoon teaching commitments on time. Finally, the Rav raised his head and suggested somewhat of a tentative solution to his *Rashi* problem. The *Shiur* was then over. Walking the Rav back to his apartment, I was curious why he could not leave this issue until the next morning's *Shiur*. So I said to him: "We know that on the second day of Creation, there's no mentioning of כי טוב (it was good), for the work of Monday was carried over to Tuesday. On that day, the כי טוב is mentioned twice – once for the completed Monday activity and one for the Tuesday work. The question is why didn't God complete His Monday work on Monday?" The Rav looked at me and said: "What do you think." I said: "I really didn't know God's reasons for doing so. But, we can conclude one thing from this: Monday's *Shiur* doesn't have to be completed on Monday, but can carry over to Tuesday, and Tuesday's *Shiur* doesn't have to be completed on Tuesday, but can carry over to Wednesday!" I received a fine homiletic grade for this comment. But, the Rav said he could not leave *Rashi* there without offering some plausible explanation.

The next morning, the Rav entered the classroom and began asking various students how well they slept the past night. Everyone seemed to have slept well. The Rav then roared that he didn't sleep well at all with that *Rashi* bothering him the whole night! He then ordered everyone to erase everything he suggested at the end of yesterday's *Shiur*. Now, he has the correct understanding, said the Rav, as he broke out in a huge smile of satisfaction. The lesson of perseverance certainly paid off.

30   Inquiry from my Younger Brother

In his high school years, my younger brother, Donny, studied at one of the famous yeshivot in Brooklyn. In eleventh grade the tractate of Talmud studied that year was *Yevamot* – one of the most difficult and intricate sections of the entire Talmud. In midyear, the students complained to their teacher that they were all drowning in the "Sea of Talmud." They begged him to make a mid-course correction and switch the tractate. The teacher asked them: "So what would you like to learn?" The boys responded: "*Berakhot*" (the laws of recitation of *Shema*, prayer, and miscellaneous blessings). The teacher retorted: "*Berakhot*?? That's for summer camp learning groups!!"

My brother asked me to get the Rav's opinion on this educational matter. I, indeed, brought this story to the Rav's attention. He reacted immediately that this teacher is completely out of line! He, himself, dedicated two years (1953–1954) at YU engaged in the in-depth analytical study of *Berakhot*. He agreed with my brother and his classmates that *Yevamot* was clearly not for them.

The Talmud (*Avoda Zara* 19b) relates that even the mundane talk of Torah scholars must be studied. (אפילו שיחת חולין של תלמידי חכמים צריכה תלמוד) The Rav was not a person with whom one could have an idle chat. The content of any discussion with the Rav was Torah-oriented. While it would be fair to say that throughout his lifetime, the Rav was engrossed in Torah, he was definitely not blind to general culture surrounding his environment and era. Although rare, the Rav could blurt out something of a very mundane nature (שיחת חולין).

R' Mendi Gopin,[7] relates a story of him reading the sports section of The New York Times on a *Yom Tov* morning in the Maimonides School Synagogue. Standing over his shoulder and glancing at the paper was, of all people, the Rav! R' Gopin writes that the Rav relieved his embarrassment by telling him, "My grandchildren would kill me if I didn't know the score."

I got a momentary glimpse of the Rav's awareness of the baseball results. It was in October, 1975, the Rav's hometown team, the Boston Red Sox, was playing the sixth game of a four of seven World Series game. The opposing team, the Cincinnati Reds, was leading the series three games to two. For the Boston team, it was "do or die" in this sixth game. At the YU Morgenstern dormitory, there was one television in the basement hall available for students. On this evening, the room was filled to (beyond) capacity with not only native Bostonians, but many other YU

7. *Davening with the Rav*, 2006, pp. 24–25.

students who had an affinity to Boston. The game turned out to be one of the most dramatic games in baseball history ending in a twelfth-inning "walk-off" homerun winning the game for Boston and moving the series to a final seventh game. The next morning, everyone at YU was buzzing about this game. At the Rav's *Shiur*, it was business as usual. The Rav completed the *Shiur* after over two hours in the classroom. As usual, I would escort the Rav back to his apartment. As he was fumbling with his keys to open the door, he turned around to me and said: "What a game!" I was so dumbfounded by the comment that I reacted in a Shakespearean manner: "et tu Brute?" The Rav went on to tell me that this baseball "*narishkeit*" (nonsense) is important in connecting with his grandchildren.

This attitude of the Rav would ultimately assist me in my relationship with non-religious Israeli soldiers.

32   Torah Study Can Take Place Anywhere

The Rav believed whole-heartedly that Torah study is not limited to a particular location. While it may be more conducive to study Torah at a particular *Bet Midrash* (study hall) and with a specific teacher wherever he may be, it is not the geographic location that is important.

After the Six-day War of 1967, it became fashionable for American young men and women to spend a year or two in an Israeli Torah institution after high school. To many Yeshiva high school principals, this fad morphed into a declared educational goal. The exposure to Israeli life for a sustained time makes them likely candidates for eventual *Aliya* to Israel. The total involvement in Torah studies during this time allows these students to return with an upgraded resolve to remain Torah-committed Jews, which incorporates Torah study on some regular basis.

The Rav appreciated the value of students studying for a time in Israel during their college years. However, he totally negated the idea that only in *Eretz Yisrael* could one fully appreciate the Torah. His proof came from the *Yom Kippur* service of the High Priest, at one point descending from the area of the Temple per se and reading the Torah in the "woman's gallery" portion of the Temple Mount (Rambam, *Hilkhot Avodat Yom HaKippurim* 3:10). Why would the High Priest not remain in the Temple area for the ceremonial Torah reading? The Rav suggested that this was to teach us the vital lesson that Torah study need not take place in areas that enjoy more sanctity than in other places. Torah is applicable to any place and can be studied in any place.

33   Positive Evil Inclinations

I recall as a fourth-grader studying Mishnah Tractate Berakhot. At that tender age, we thought that we understood everything being taught. So it was for the Mishnah Berakhot 9:5, ואהבת את ה' א-להיך בכל לבבך.... בשני יצריך ביצר טוב וביצר רע. (You shall love God with all your heart.... with your good inclination and with your evil inclination.) Only much later in life did I realize that this relatively simple Mishnah is enormously difficult to understand. The difficulty lies in the fact that we are told to love God not only with our "good inclination," but also with our "evil inclination." Loving God with one's "good inclination" is perfectly understandable. However, how does one go about loving God with one's "evil inclination"? Are we not taught to do battle against the "evil inclination"? (*Berakhot* 5a, לעולם ירגיז אדם יצר טוב על יצר הרע, and Rashi.)

I posed this question to the Rav who responded immediately that there is a basic misunderstanding regarding the יצר הרע – that "evil inclination." This "evil inclination" is not intrinsically evil. It has all the potential to lead to evil. But, in itself, it's not evil. The "evil inclination," explained the Rav, governs man's aspirations, drives, ambitions, goals, talents, and most importantly – his creativity. If cultivated properly in the direction of the Service of God (עבודת ה'), it is then considered loving God with the "evil inclination." As a matter of fact, the real challenge in the Service of God has little to do with the use of one's "good inclination." That ought to work naturally with everyone. The question is how well does one direct artistic talents to the adorning of

Mitzvah objects (הידור מצוה), or how does one use his musical talents to inspire Prayer? These are just some examples of loving God with one's "evil inclination."

> See R' Dr. Norman Lamm's *z"l* personal story in his forward remarks to the *Sefer HaYovel* (in honor of the Rav), 1984, p. 8, relating to the Rav castigating him for coming to the *Shiur* with his "good inclination" only, while leaving his "evil inclination" outside behind the closed door!

It would be fair to say that the Rav did more to legitimize Torah study for women than any other Rabbi of his generation. In 1937, the founding of the Maimonides School in Boston by the Rav and his wife, Tonya, ushered in an era of co-educational instruction in both Torah and general subjects from the first until the twelfth grade. Two independent – but related – issues were at stake. One had to do with the teaching of boys and girls together in one classroom setting, and the other was the very core issue of teaching Torah to females.

On the first issue, the Rav's opinion is unclear. Contradictory reports have surfaced, throughout the years, as to what exactly the Rav had in mind when instituting co-ed classes at Maimonides. R' Hershel Schachter reports[8] that this policy was nothing but a concession to the realities of the day. Boston's small Orthodox community at the time could not financially sustain separate Torah institutions for boys and for girls. Either the girls would study with the boys or they would receive no Torah education at all. And, the Rav made the choice to offer the girls a Torah education.

A completely different picture emerges when speaking to other members of the Rav's family and close students. For example, in conversation with the Rav's daughter, in 1995, Dr. Atara Twersky told me that her father "was the greatest feminist of the century when it came to *Talmud Torah*." The

---

8. *Nefesh HaRav*, 1994, p. 237.

Rav's feeling was that if the girls would receive separate Torah education, they would necessarily receive an inferior education. The only way to guarantee that girls received the superior Torah education that they deserved was to teach them in an integrated classroom setting with boys. Regarding the social issues, during the teenage years, the teachers would have to apply themselves in order to guarantee proper and appropriate relationships between the boys and girls in and out of school.

> In a Letter to the Editor, *Tradition* (31:3), 1997, pp. 115–116, R' Menachem Meier (Associate Principal, Maimonides School, August, 1967–July, 1971; and my Principal, The Frisch School, 1977–1979) writes: "Maimonides School was co-educational in all subjects, *kodesh* and *hol*, from primary school through the twelfth grade. The Rav visited the school frequently, saw his children and grandchildren study and develop there, and took an active role in defining and promoting the mission of the school. Never did he suggest that boys and girls be separated in any classes. Such a suggestion from the Rav would undoubtedly have been honored as he was revered by the officers and Board of Maimonides School who considered it a privilege to serve on the Board of the Rav's school.
>
> "The co-educational nature of Maimonides School leaves many, even avowed disciples of the Rav, uncomfortable. Contrary to reasons offered in certain quarters, I understood that the Rav viewed co-education not as a Halakhic issue but rather as an educational question, one to to be examined – by each community – through the prism of sound educational philosophy and tested in the laboratory of life."

The Rav was a great believer in Torah education for women. In his own home, his daughters, from a young age, were taught Torah. The crown jewel of this belief would be exhibited publicly in 1976, as the Rav inaugurated the new-formed *Bet Midrash* program at Stern College for Women (YU), by delivering the opening *Shiur* in Talmud. The moment was not only historic for the school, but also for all the women – young and old – clamoring for the opportunity to be exposed to the Talmud on a serious level. Many of the women studying Talmud regularly at the wonderful *Batei Midrash* for women, both in the United States and in Israel, owe a great debt of thanks to the Rav for his bold pioneering step taken that day at Stern College. The next morning, I asked the Rav how he felt about being a "revolutionary." "A revolutionary!" he exclaimed. "I'm not a revolutionary. Sarah Shneirer *z"l* [founder, in 1917, of the first Bais Yaakov school in Crakow, Poland with the blessings of the Rebbe of Ger, the Rebbe of Belz, and the Hafetz Hayim]; she was the revolutionary. From then on, the only question remaining was that of syllabus. Today, a young woman has all academic options open to her. We see no reason today not to teach her Talmud."[9]

The Rav was obviously not oblivious to the Halakhic sources exempting women from Torah study (Rambam, *Hilkhot Talmud Torah* 1:1, נשים ועבדים וקטנים פטורים מתלמוד תורה). He did believe that while women may enjoy a partial exemption from Torah study within the framework of the commandment to study Torah, they are not at all exempt from the commandment to love God,[10] a commandment whose fulfillment requires serious Torah study.

An interesting postscript to these conversations occurred in 1979, prior to my *Aliya* to Israel. My wife, Miriam, and three-year old daughter, Ahuva, came to meet me once in the lobby of Furst Hall at YU. When the Rav exited at that moment from the elevator, I told my daughter: "Go say hello to the Rav." She ran towards the elevator waving her hand and saying: "Hi Wav!" The Rav looked down and said: "What's this? We're bringing little girls to the Bet Midrash?" I asked the Rav if he had any objections. To which the Rav responded: "No, no. It's okay. When our Sages

---

9. See R' Hershel Schachter, *Mipnenei HaRav*, 2001, pp. 167–168.
10. Rambam, *Hilkhot Teshuva* 10:5–6.

spoke about R' Yehoshua b. Hanania, אשרי יולדתו – ["worthy is the one who gave birth to him" – the Sages reported that R' Yehoshua's mother took him as an infant to the Bet Midrash to absorb the music of Torah study] this applies to little girls as well!"

Indeed, Ahuva – today a mother and teacher - is deeply engrossed in Torah study!

The Rav, speaking often about Torah study, would relate to the Aggadic statement (Talmud, *Niddah* 30b) that every embryo is taught all of Torah and then, by an angelic slap in the face, the newborn instantaneously fogets it all. The purpose is that all of our Torah study is nothing but recall of previously acquired knowledge allowing us some measure of grasping the Divine Word.[11] The Rav once told me that this Aggadic tradition makes no distinction between male and female embryos. The girls were "exposed" in utero to "all of Torah" no less than the boys!

11. See "Redemption, Prayer, and Talmud Torah," *Tradition* (17 no. 2), 1978, pp. 68–69.

Driving from LaGuardia Airport one Tuesday morning, I gave thought to the subject matter to be dealt with in that evening's *Shiur* at Congregation Moriah in midtown Manhattan. (See Conversation #53). The Talmud, *Sukkah* 46a, states the following:

תנו רבנן: היו לפניו מצות הרבה, אומר: ברוך אשר קדשנו במצותיו וצונו על המצות. רבי יהודה אומר: מברך על כל אחת ואחת בפני עצמה. אמר רבי זירא ואיתימא רבי חנינא בר פפא: **הלכתא כרבי יהודה.** ואמר רבי זירא ואיתימא רבי חנינא בר פפא: מאי טעמא דרבי יהודה דכתיב ברוך ה' יום יום, וכי ביום מברכין אותו ובלילה אין מברכין אותו? אלא בא לומר לך: בכל יום ויום תן לו מעין ברכותיו, הכא נמי בכל דבר ודבר תן לו מעין ברכותיו. ואמר רבי זירא ואיתימא רבי חנינא בר פפא: בא וראה שלא כמדת הקדוש ברוך הוא מדת בשר ודם; מדת בשר ודם, כלי ריקן מחזיק, מלא אינו מחזיק, אבל מדת הקדוש ברוך הוא: מלא מחזיק, ריקן אינו מחזיק, שנאמר והיה אם שמוע תשמע וגו' אם שמוע – תשמע, ואם לאו – לא תשמע. דבר אחר: אם שמוע בישן – תשמע בחדש, ואם יפנה לבבך – שוב לא תשמע.

Our Rabbis taught, He who has to perform many commandments (simultaneously) shall say, "Blessed . . . who hast sanctified us by Thy commandments." R' Judah ruled, one must recite a benediction over each one separately. R' Zera or, as some say, R' Hanina b. Papa stated: **The Halakha is in agreement with R' Judah.**

The Talmud goes on to explain the basis for R' Judah's opinion, and then follows with an Aggadic portion contrasting the ways of God as opposed to human behavior.

A parallel section – almost verbatim – appears in Berakhot 40a regarding a dispute between the Sages and R' Judah over the proper blessing over diverse kinds of herbs. The rationale in both Talmudic sources for R' Judah's view is identical. Yet, in the second source, it reads: "The Halakha is **not** in agreement with R' Judah (אין הלכה כרבי יהודה).[12]

I raised the question to the Rav, if the rationale for R' Judah's opinion in both disputes was identical, why then would the Halakha accept R' Judah's opinion in one case and reject it in the other? The Rav granted me permission to suggest an answer. I said that the answer lies in the Aggadic material that followed the Halakhic discussion (all in the name of the same author!) It had to do with the difference of character between the ways of God and human behavior. When performing commandments – the more the merrier. Therefore, one could recite multiple blessings over various commandments. Whereas when it comes to human consumption of food, there are physical limits. Therefore, we should not exaggerate with excessive blessings. The Rav nodded, but said no more.

That evening at Moriah, the Rav began his *Shiur* with the words (in Yiddish): "מיין דרייבער האט געפרעגט" ("My driver asked...". I must confess that this was a thrilling moment for me. But to my dismay, while the Rav reported my question to the audience, he followed up with a completely different answer

---

12. A variant Talmudic reading, connoting the exact opposite decision (והלכה כר"י) is preserved in R' Refoel Natan Rabinowitz's *Dikdukei Sofrim* to Berakhot 40a. This reading actually concurs with the Sukkah 46a source, thus negating this very conversation. However, as I once heard from my Rebbe, R' Hershel Schachter, variant readings are to be treated as authentic Torah and not merely as "scribal errors" (טעות סופרים). Hence, this conversation – along with the Rav's understanding – remains firm on solid ground.

based upon Halakhic principles rather than on the Aggadic material as I had suggested.[13]

> Morris Laub, a regular attendee of the Rav's Tuesday evening *Shiur* at Moriah Congregation, penned a beautiful letter in the American Jewish Congress' *Congress By-Weekly*, November 12, 1971, describing the inspirational experience enjoyed by all attendees of the *Shiur*. The Rav's equally beautiful response can be seen in Rabbi Joseph B. Soloveitchik's *Community, Covenant, and Commitment*, (Ed. Nathaniel Helfgot), 2005, pp. 337–338.

13. See *Reshimat Shiurim (Sukkah) of R' Yosef Dov Halevi Soloveitchik*, (ed. R' Zvi Reichman), 1989, p. 245.

The Rav meeting the newly-elected Prime Minister of Israel, Menachem Begin, 1977. (*Photo: Ya'akov Sa'ar; Credits: Photo Department, Israel Government Press Office*)

Rav entering dinner hall with honoree Joseph Gruss. On the right: Rav's son-in-law, R' Yitzhak Twersky zt"l. On the left: R' Jay Marcus.
(*Photo: R'Aharon Ziegler*)

III _____ Israel and the Jewish Nation

You say, for instance, that "all Jews are friends" [Prayer for the New Month], that all Jews are united. When the Jews observe the mitzvot, I can understand this thought that we are united and friends.... Today... I cannot comprehend the concept. By what virtue are they joined together? ... If there is no observance of mitzvot, the last bond between Jews will disappear. This is why Rambam stressed the serious consequences of not joining the Jewish community in the performance of the mitzvot and in the houses of worship and study. There are unifying forces and factors which enable us to be one people ... when we come to the prayer [for the New Month] "that our dispersed will be ingathered from the four corners of the earth in the fellowship of all Israel," then the Torah scroll should be held aloft. This prayer stresses the unity of the Jewish people. It is the Sefer Torah which unites us....

— The Rav, ed. R' Aaron Rakefet-Rothkoff, Vol. I, 1999, pp. 189–190

I will never forget the evening in 5695 [1935] when I visited Rabbi [Zev] Gold in Ramat Gan in Eretz Yisrael. He took me out to the orange groves near his house. It was a beautiful night, the sky was perfectly blue and there were endless stars.... From afar we could see the lights of the new all-Jewish city of Tel Aviv glistening in the dark. The lights were telling us the thrilling and intoxicating news of the rebuilding of the Holy Land.... As we stood there, R' Gold picked up a small pebble and kissed it, to fulfill Rav Abba's dictum in the Talmud that he would kiss the rocks of Akko [Ketubot 112a]. That night, I thought to myself how insignificant I was compared to this special Jew who was able to experience the glory of God through the grandeur of the landscape of the land of Israel.

— The Rav, ed. R' Aaron Rakefet-Rothkoff, Vol. 2, 1999, p. 118

The Rav's manifesto on Religious Zionism in general, and on the national need for increased *Aliya* to Israel in particular, was eloquently articulated in his 1956 *Yom Ha'Atzma'ut* address at YU entitled, *Kol Dodi Dofek.* Subsequently, this speech, originally delivered in Yiddish, was printed in both Hebrew and in English translations. In his capacity as Hon. President of the Religious Zionists of America (Mizrahi), the Rav would deliver a keynote address at the organization's annual convention. Many of these speeches appeared in book form entitled, "*The Rav Speaks.*" It is clear to all who heard or read these talks that the Rav had a very positive outlook on *Aliya.*

> The Rav told me that he never liked the word, "Diaspora," because it lent legitimacy to those living outside of *Eretz Yisrael.* The appropriate word should be "*Galut*" (exile), giving one the sense of detachment from one's home. Without a constant sensation of "*Galut,*" there could be no longing for *Aliya* to Israel.

Yet, when it came to his own students who occupied positions in the rabbinate and/or education, the Rav was far less enthusiastic – to say the least.[1]

In March, 1977, I began my tenure as a community Rabbi at Congregation Sons of Israel in Long Island City, N.Y., and concurrently served as a teacher of Jewish Studies at The Frisch

1. See R' Hershel Schachter, *Divrei HaRav,* 2010, p. 219.

School in Paramus, N.J. I shared my *Aliya* ambitions with the
Rav during the course of 1978. I felt all along that I had to fight
to obtain a proper blessing from the Rav prior to our expected
Aliya in July, 1979. In fact, it became increasingly evident that
the Rav was hopeful that his students would recognize their
national responsibility to do God's work on American soil.

My Jewish Agency-sponsored pilot trip coincided with
Hanukah of 1978. I argued that in the dispute between the *Bet
Shammai* and *Bet Hillel* schools regarding the order of candle
lighting – from eight to one or from one to eight – the Talmud
(Shabbat 21b) refers to *Bet Shammai's* view as פוחת והולך
(descending order), as opposed to the view of *Bet Hillel* that of
מוסיף והולך (ascending order). When considering the future of
the Jewish people, with intermarriage and assimilation running
at alarming rates, it's clear that the American scene is a פוחת
והולך situation, while Jewish population growth can be seen in
the State of Israel as a מוסיף והולך scenario. As we all know, the
Halakha is in accordance with *Bet Hillel*! I, therefore, argued
that my future should be with the future of our people.

I referred to a *Shiur* delivered by the Rav before *Pesah*, based
upon the *Haggadah* story of the *Seder* in *Bnei Brak*. The Rav
homiletically explained that the Torah giants (גדולי תורה) of each
generation are deeply concerned throughout the long night of
exile about the fate of the nation והיו מספרין ביציאת מצרים כל אותו
הלילה. I asked the Rav permission for me to continue on this
homiletic line: עד שבאו תלמידיהם ואמרו להם רבותינו הגיע זמן קרית שמע
של שחרית. It would ultimately be the students – not the teachers
– who would usher in the redemptive era. And I saw myself as
part of that crowd of students.

On another occasion, I recall quoting the Talmudic ruling[2]
that: לעולם ידור אדם בא"י אפי' בעיר שרובה גוים, ואל ידור בחו"ל ואפילו
בעיר שרובה ישראל. "It is always preferable to reside in *Eretz
Yisrael* even in a city with a gentile majority, rather than living

2. *Ketubot* 110b, and quoted verbatim by Rambam in *Hilkhot
Melakhim* 5:9.

in the Diaspora in a city with a Jewish majority." I suggested to the Rav that if we plug in modern day coordinates to this ruling, we could say that it would be preferable to live in Nazareth – an Israeli city with a guaranteed non-Jewish majority – rather than live in Monsey, N.Y, in a heavily-populated Jewish community. My occupational possibilities in Nazareth would include, perhaps, driving an Egged bus or working as a plumber, while in Monsey, there would surely be opportunities in the rabbinate and/or education. Yet, the Talmudic ruling speaks of לעולם (always) in talking about residing in *Eretz Yisrael* irrespective of vocational consequences! To this, the Rav remarked: "It's a very nice *Drasha*!"

The Rav then voiced his concerns that I may not "find" myself in Israel, and that it would be a waste losing me in America. He assured me that in twenty years' time, I would be elected President of the Rabbinical Council of America (RCA). To which I retorted, with as much respect as I could muster, "Does the Rav have any other 'blessings' up his sleeve?" Finally, I promised the Rav that no matter what I would be doing in Israel, I would try my utmost not to embarrass his good name.

I recall, at the time, telling the Rav that I thank God for being a *talmid* of the Rav and not a *Hassid* of the Rav.

> In Hassidic circles, the Rebbe's "advice" was a determining factor on personal decisions. The Rav never wanted to serve in such a capacity. He believed that his students had the right to decide on personal matters even against his "advice." As a matter of fact, the Rav had an overall negative opinion on the doctrine of "*Da'at Torah*" (דעת תורה) – the attitude developed by R' Elhanan Wasserman הי"ד and the Hafetz Haim zt"l – which grants talmudic scholars "Torah wisdom" in general areas of life such as medical issues, politics, and the weather. Questioning the Rav on his thoughts concerning "*Da'at Torah*," he responded: "When you figure it out, come back and tell me."[3]

3. On the evolution of the "*Da'at Torah*" doctrine, see Binyamim Brown,

On July 1, 1979, en route to JFK Airport beginning a new life for myself and for my young family in Israel, I received a warm telephone greeting and blessing from the Rav; he requested of me to keep him abreast of my undertakings.

פולמוס, דעת תורה, בציונית הדתית בישראל – הרקע, העמדות והמשמעויות; *Religious Zionism: an Era of Changes* (Hebrew), 2004, pp. 422–474.

37

Hallel on Yom Ha'Atzma'ut – an Official Position

The Rav's position regarding the recitation of *Hallel* on Israel's Independence Day (יום העצמאות) is somewhat ambiguous. Many have claimed to have witnessed the Rav do this or that (full *Hallel*, half *Hallel*, before the *Kaddish*, after the *Kaddish*, etc.).[4] Some have suggested that this ambiguity demonstrated a less-than-enthusiastic attitude towards the State itself.[5]

> Commenting upon the Rav's so-called ambiguity on Religious Zionism, the Rav's daughter, Dr. Tova Lichtenstein, told me that when the book, *On Repentance* (Hebrew) was published in Jerusalem in 1974, it was awarded a prize for outstanding Torah literature. Dr. Lichtenstein, knowing fully well that her father would not accept the prize money personally, asked him where he would prefer to contribute this money. The response was: "Give it to Rav Neriah for the Yeshivot Bnei Akiva." Dr. Lichtenstein continued that this immediate answer from the Rav didn't sound like someone grappling with ambiguous feeling towards Religious Zionism!

4. For a full overview, see R' Shmuel Katz, *The Chief Rabbinate of Israel – 70 Years Since its Foundation*, 2002, Vol. 2, (Hebrew), pp. 950–1, Notes 153–6. See also R' Hershel Schachter, *Divrei HaRav*, 2010, pp. 175–6.

5. Negating this point vehemently, see R' Aharon Lichtenstein, "The Relationship of the Gaon R' Yosef Dov Soloveitchik to Zionism," (Hebrew) in 2012, חמש דרשות.

During the mid-1970s, the doctoral dissertation of R' Louis Bernstein was accepted by the Bernard Revel Graduate School of Yeshiva University. (See Conversation #43). This academic work dealt with the impact of the Rabbinical Council of America (RCA) on the formation of modern Orthodoxy in America.[6]

This dissertation contained an appendix with eight printed Halakhic responsa from the Rav (as Chairman of the Halakha Commision) to the Executive Director and officers of the RCA. They were all questions dealing with public policy on the part of the RCA. One question dated in the early 1950s, sought the Rav's opinion regarding the reaction and proper procedures of the RCA towards Israel's Independence Day. Specifically, should *Hallel* be recited or not? The extremely brief four Hebrew word response of the Rav was: "They said and they said" הם אמרו והם אמרו.

In conversation, I asked the Rav what he meant by using this Talmudic phrase? (In Talmudic terms, the phrase, הם אמרו והם אמרו means that the Sages who ordained a restriction also had the authority to relax this restriction in specific cases.)[7] The Rav responded that he had nothing to do with the establishment of Israel's Independence Day. It was the Chief Rabbinate of Israel that instituted the saying *Hallel* that day. Therefore, הם אמרו – they said it – that there should be a holiday, so הם אמרו – they have the authority to say what should be done or said on that day. The Rav explained that this was not a private Halakhic inquiry, but rather one of public nature. Since the question as such emanated from Israel, the Chief Rabbinate must serve as the Resident Rabbinic authority (מרא דאתרא) on this case.

> In conversation with R' Aharon Lichtenstein *zt"l*, I was told that the Rav did not grant the Israeli Chief Rabbinate מרא דאתרא status on all subjects. But he did agree that on questions regarding

---

6. The published book version, *Challenge and Mission: the Emergence of the English-speaking Orthodox Rabbinate*, appeared in 1982.

7. See, for example, Mishnah Yoma 8:1 and Tosefot Yom Tov.

Hallel on Israel's Independence Day, the Chief Rabbinate did serve in this function. So, too, regarding the Rav's opinion on the personal status of the Ethiopian Jewish community immigrating to Israel in the 1980s, the Rav thought that the RCA should follow the instructions of the Israeli Chief Rabbinate. (See Conversation #70.)

In his *Davening with the Rav*, 2006, p. 115, R' Mendi Gopin reports on the custom in Boston's Maimonides School *Minyan*: "On Yom Haatzmut to recite the *whole Hallel* without a *brochoh*, and on Yom Yerushalayim to recite *whole Hallel* with a *brochoh* at the beginning and the end." This is completely in line with the Rav's directives to the Rabbinical Council of America from the 1950s.[8]

It should be pointed out, however, that privately the Rav did not say *Hallel* with a *brakha* on Yom Yerushalayim, nor did he ever encourage others to do so.

8. See also, Yitzchok Levine discussing this subject on "The Avodah Mailing List," Vol. 27, #104, April 21, 2010.

38

Reacting to Menachem Begin's Election (1977)

In May, 1977, Menachem Begin won the Israeli Elections causing an upheaval in Israeli politics. (In the words of Israel TV anchorman, Hayim Yavin: מהפך!) For the first time in nineteen years, the country would not be governed by Israel's Labor Party. The Rav had a personal affinity for, and camaraderie with Menachem Begin who hailed from Brisk (Brest-Litovsk). The Rav told me that in Israel we previously had five *Israeli* Prime Ministers (David Ben Gurion, Moshe Sharett, Levi Eshkol, Golda Meir, and Yitzhak Rabin). We finally now have a *Jewish* Prime Minister!

39   The 1977 Rav/Menachem Begin Meeting

During the early summer of 1977, the newly-elected Prime Minister of Israel, Menachem Begin, made an official visit to the United States. During his short stay in a New York City Hotel, the Prime Minister wished to consult with three great Torah leaders regarding certain issues on the religious/political agenda. Among other things, was the question of moving Holocaust Memorial Day (יום השואה והגבורה) from the 27th of Nissan to the Fast of the 9th of Av. The three Torah leaders included R' Menachem Mendel Schneerson – the Rebbe of Habad, R' Moshe Feinstein, and the Rav. The first two resided in New York. Hence, it was easy for Begin to visit them on their premises. However, during the summer months, the Rav did not come into New York. Yet, when it was brought to the Rav's attention that the Prime Minister wished to meet him, he was prepared to make a special trip from Boston to New York for this occasion. The Rav reasoned that the Halakah of showing honor to the polilitical leadership (כבוד המלכות) demanded of him to take this step.[9] When Begin heard of this, he felt it only right for him to make the trip to Boston, for he said that the Rav was the "*Gedol HaDor*" (the greatest of the generation). To which the Rav responded that if Begin views him as the "*Gedol HaDor*," then he is Halakhically deciding that *he* must go to see Begin – and not the other way around! And, the Rav did just that. (Details heard directly from R' Israel Miller *z"l*). The

---

9. Rambam, *Hilkhot Melakhim* 2:1.

Rav remarked to me that, in a way, he was correcting (תיקון)
the episode found in *Tosephot, Ta'anit* 4a, regarding that which
took place between the Judge, *Yiftah* and *Pinhas*.

> Regarding the transfer of Holocaust Memorial Day to the 9th
> of Av, all three of the Torah leaders responded positively to the
> suggestion. However, the idea was summarily rejected by Israel's
> Ministry of Education on the grounds that during the summer
> vacation months proper Holocaust studies and memorials could
> not take place. I heard this personally from Israel's Minister of
> Education, Mr. Zevulun Hammer *a"h*.
>
> In general, the Rav believed that discussion of the Holocaust
> should, indeed, take place within the context of reciting the
> existing elegies (קינות) composed in medieval times. This view is in
> conformity with the Talmudic statement (*Ta'anit* 29a) that the 9th
> of Av has been designated as the day of בכייה לדורות ("perpetual
> crying").[10] The Rav took sharp objection to the composing of
> modern-day elegies for the Holocaust. He writes (p. 299): "I just
> do not believe that a contemporary has the inner ability, the faith,
> the depth, the sweep of experience, the ecstasy, the *taharat ha-
> nefesh*, the purity of soul, that would authorize him or give him
> permission to write a *piyut*. I just do not believe that there is
> anyone today who is qualified to do this." Ironically, the excellent
> edition of the Elegies for the Ninth of Av, with the Rav's running
> commentary, contains four such Holocaust elegies recited in
> many Synagogues throughout the world today.[11]

---

10. See Rabbi Joseph B. Soloveitchik, *The Lord is Righteous in All His
Ways*, ed. R' J.J. Schacter, 2006, pp. 289–301.

11. See *The Koren Mesorat Harav Kinot*, (ed. R' Simon Posner), 2010, pp.
620–639.

The first serious opportunity the Rav had to immigrate to *Eretz Yisrael* was when he applied for the position of Ashkenazi Chief Rabbi of Tel Aviv in 1935. This would be the only time the Rav ever visited the Holy Land. At the time, the Rav – a young and not-well known personality in Palestine – was the Agudat Yisrael candidate. He faced the favorite R' Moshe Avigdor Amiel *z"l* from Antwerp, Belgium – the Mizrahi candidate. Although the Rav invested much energy in his campaign during his several months' visit, he severely lost the election.

The next opportunity for the Rav presented itself immediately after the passing of Israel's second Ashkenazi Chief Rabbi, R' Yitzchak Isaac Herzog *zt"l* in 1959. The Rav's name – by then a world-renowned Torah figure – surfaced as a serious candidate to succeed R' Herzog. After months of soul-searching and deliberation, the Rav removed himself from the race. Many people questioned the Rav, throughout the years, concerning his motives for not accepting the position. The Rav furnished many people with many different answers! On one occasion, I asked the Rav if the opposition of his uncle (R' Velvele Soloveitchik *zt"l*, the Brisker Rav) was the critical reason for his not accepting the position. The Rav responded that while it was true that his uncle opposed his accepting the position, this was not the critical point. In the final analysis, the Rav continued, the authority of Israel's Chief Rabbi does not emanate from the *Shulhan Arukh*, but rather from the Law of Israel's Knesset. Therefore, the Chief Rabbi's hands are tied. He cannot say what he wants to say, when he wants to say it, and how he wants to say it! The Rav said that he had the greatest respect for those who occupied the position in the past. But, a rabbinate not fully independent was not for him.

Finally, the Rav quipped: in all the government offices in Israel, there are photos hanging on the walls of all the predecessors of that office. So, too, in the Chief Rabbis offices, you can see such photos. The Rav continued: I don't think I would have a problem being on the wall with Rav Kook or Rav Herzog. I do worry that I may have problems being on the wall with those who will come afterwards many years later!

> In two 1960-dated letters – one to Israel's Interior Minister Chaim Moshe Shapira z"l and the other to Petah Tivkva's Chief Rabbi Reuven Katz z"l – the Rav "officially" explains his reasons for withdrawing his candidacy from the race for the position of Chief Rabbi in Israel.[12]

---

12. See Rabbi Joseph B. Soloveitchik, ed. Nathaniel Helfgot, *Community, Covenant, and Commitment*, 2005, pp. 173–177.

112

Issue of "Who is a Jew"

Israel's first Knesset Law in 1950 – The Law of Return – guaranteed all Jews the right to immigrate to Israel and immediately to become citizens. Since that date, the governments of Israel have been struggling with an acceptable working definition of "Who is a Jew." The law reads that a Jew is a person born to a Jewish mother or converted to Judaism. The Israeli religious parties have been working tediously to amend the law to specifically limit conversions to Halakhic conversions.[13]

> In a humoristic note, the Rav told me that one does not have to consult the *Shulhan Arukh* for the definition of "Who is a Jew." One must only ask a local anti-Semite, and he will, for sure, supply you an answer that certainly would be לחומרא (strict interpretation)!! This bit of humor seems to be implied by the Talmudic statement (Megillah 13b): גלוי וידוע לפני מי שאמר והיה העולם שעתיד המן לשקול שקלים על ישראל, לפיכך הקדים שקליהן לשקליו.

In 1976, a rumor spread that the then Prime Minister of Israel, Yitzhak Rabin, was prepared to offer the National Religious Party a deal that would include dropping their political demands

13. Regarding the "Who is a Jew"? issue, see the Rav's 1959 response (jointly with R' Chayim Heller *zt"l*) to Prime Minister Ben Gurion and joint letter by the Rav and R' Moshe Feinstein in Rabbi Joseph B. Soloveitchik, ed. Nathaniel Helfgot, *Community, Covenant, and Commitment*, 2005, pp. 167–172.

to amend this law in exchange for the Education Minister portfolio. The Rav reacted that, in his opinion, if true, he would recommend closing such a deal with Rabin. His thinking was that the dangers of a handful of converts from the Conservative or Reform movements immigrating to Israel were marginal. He felt confident that the Chief Rabbinate could deal with these individual cases. However, the prospect of having a religious Minister of Education could impact positively upon an entire generation!

In conversation years later with Dr. Zerah Warhaftig z"l (former Minister of Religious Affairs) and me, he categorically denied the rumor of such a pending offer by Rabin. However, he agreed with the Rav that, in theory, this would have been a good deal.

In retrospect, after having several Ministers of Education from the national/religious sector, it is fair to say that the Rav was overly optimistic in his positive assessments regarding what a religious Minister of Education could possibly accomplish.

42   A Vote for Gerald Ford (1976)

In the Presidential elections of 1976 between the Republican incumbent, Gerald Ford and his Democratic challenger, Jimmy Carter, most American Jews voted for Jimmy Carter. Aside from the general affiliation of Jews with the Democratic Party, in this particular election there was a sense that President Ford's Secretary of State, Henry Kissenger, had unnecessarily and unfairly pressured Israel in the 1974–75 Disengagement Talks with Syria.

Yet, the Rav confided in me that he opted to vote for Ford, going against the whims of most American Jews. His rationale was that Jimmy Carter was a devout Christian, while Ford was a *"sheigetz"* (categorically NOT a religious man). Throughout history, the Jewish people suffered from religious zealots and extremists. The Rav preferred not seeing such a devoutly religious Christian, such as Jimmy Carter, in the White House.

> With the passing of time, the former President Carter exhibited his true colors with his vehemently anti-Israel political positions.

43

In 1976, R' Louis Bernstein z"l, the veteran Rabbi, educator, and Jewish leader, was elected to the Presidency of the Religious Zionists of America (Mizrahi). I was present when R' Bernstein arrived at the Rav's door to receive his blessings upon taking office in this important undertaking. The Rav advised R' Bernstein that from all of the wonderful Mizrahi accomplishments, the one that should overshadow all the others was the proliferation of the Yeshivot Bnei Akiva and the Yeshivot Hesder. The rehabilitation and growth of Torah in a Religious Zionist atmosphere stood at the core of the Mizrahi movement. The Rav told R' Bernstein that if all that he were to accomplish during his tenure in office was the successful promotion of these Mizrahi-based institutions, then דיינו (it would be sufficient)!

> The Rav's overall positive attitude towards the Yeshivat Hesder model (combining Torah study with military service) can be seen in the following story:
>
> In the mid-1970s, the Rav was visited by the then Chief Chaplain of the Israeli army, R' Gad Navon z"l. The very first comment of the Rav to R' Navon was that he had a grandson, a "tankist" (referring to R' Moshe Lichtenstein who was serving at the time, in the Israeli army's armored corps)! This was, indeed, a very proud grandfather speaking!
>
> Another fascinating anecdote demonstrating the Rav's deep admiration for the Yeshivat Hesder soldier/student relates to his remarkable P'sak (Halakhic decision) regarding a Yeshivat

Har Etzion student serving in the armored corps given the tedious task of cleaning the tanks. By the time he completed his task, his uniform was thoroughly dirtied with grease and grime. He then noticed that sundown was rapidly approaching and time was running short for *Minha*. The question was would he necessarily have to change his soiled clothing and be more properly dressed for davening? This soldier's query was brought to the Rav's attention (by visiting R' Aharon Lichtenstein *zt"l*), who immediately responded: "I don't understand the question; Israeli army uniforms are *bigdei kodesh* (holy garments)!"

The name, Joseph Gruss *a"h*, is iconic in the world of Jewish philanthropy. By the 1970s, it was reported that Mr. Gruss had donated in excess of one hundred million dollars to a variety of Jewish institutionally-funded causes. In relating to me this tidbit of information, the Rav said that Mr. Gruss still had some change left over!

The Rav began to unravel a tale of how Mr. Gruss morphed into one of the all-time giants in Torah-institution philanthropy. This had not always been the case. While Mr. Gruss had been actively supporting Jewish Federations, hospitals, and the like, the yeshiva world was not yet on his agenda.

Mr. Gruss had a family member studying at one of Boston's finest academic institutions. At the time, this person was in need of some spiritual guidance. The family was told of a Rabbi Soloveitchik in Boston who spoke the language of the academicians, and would possibly be able to speak to this person. The Rav was approached by an intermediary. A series of three meetings between the Rav and this person were arranged which ultimately led to the full resolution of the issue at hand. The Gruss family was so appreciative that they offered the Rav a gift. Of course, the Rav would not accept a gift. (He reminded me of the severe repercussions sustained by the Biblical Gehazi in II Kings, Chapter 5, who accepted a gift on behalf of services rendered in the Name of God.) But, Mr. Gruss was adamant and wanted to do something for the Rav. So, the Rav told him that he teaches at the Rabbi Isaac Elchanan Theological Seminary

[RIETS] of Yeshiva University in New York. He would be extremely honored if Mr. Gruss left a donation at the Yeshiva. Mr. Gruss immediately wrote out a check for one million dollars to the Yeshiva! The Rav, with his sharp humor, looked at me and said: "Had I known what he was talking about.... I thought he planned to buy me a gold watch. I had one already!" But, in all seriousness, the Rav jumped at the opportunity of cultivating a friendship with Mr. Gruss that would become beneficial not only for YU, but for the entire yeshiva world in the United States. The Rav told me that Mr. Gruss brought him into the picture to convince the Federation to begin allocating funds and support for Torah education. At YU, a long-term endowment was setup by Mr. Gruss for RIETS.

> In his eulogy for the Rav entitled: "About the Rav: These Things I Remember," *Memories of a Giant*, 2003, p. 307, Dr. Alvin I. Schiff recalls: "the Rav... was a member of the initial Professional Advisory Committee of the Program Development Fund for Jewish Education (PDF), a cooperative enterprise sponsored by Joseph Gruss and The Federation of Jewish Philanthropies of New York.... The Rav came punctually and regularly to the meetings, participated actively in our deliberations and helped guide the development of the Fund for Jewish Education in Greater New York. His input was crucial in establishing allocation guidelines which eventually led to the distribution of ninety percent of the funds to *yeshivot* and day schools.... Overwhelmingly, the money was contributed by Mr. Gruss... whose admiration for the Rav knew no bounds."

In 1975, Mr. Gruss fulfilled his magnanimous pledge to Dr. Samuel Belkin *z"l*, President of YU, to erect a full campus in Jerusalem. This campus, carrying the name, "The Caroline and Joseph Gruss Institute," would house the Israel branch of the *Kollel* program. The pledge to YU carried with it a condition. The Rav had to commit to coming to Jerusalem to teach for one year to launch the Gruss Center in Jerusalem. I vividly recall a large get-together of RIETS students in 1975 at the gala announcement of the opening of the Gruss Center. The Rav was in attendance at the gathering. A student publicly called out, asking if the Rav would be joining the first group of students at the Gruss Center. He responded that if he feels healthy enough, he will spend half the year in Jerusalem. There was thunderous applause in the room! Unfortunately, this was not to be, and it left Mr. Gruss quite disappointed.

In the winter of 1976, my elementary and high school alma mater, Yeshiva & Mesivta Toras Emes Kamenitz, completed a one million dollar, Joseph Gruss-funded, building project in the Boro Park section of Brooklyn, NY. A royal dinner was held in his honor at the new yeshiva premises. At this dinner, Mr. Gruss invited all of the yeshiva heads to whose institutions he had donated money. An all-star gallery of Torah giants was present led by R' Moshe Feinstein, of Tiferet Yerushalayim (who presented Mr. Gruss with a newly-written *Sefer Torah* in his honor), R' Shneur Kotler of Lakewood, R' Kalmanovich of Mir זכרונם לברכה, along with many others. At the dinner, all the Torah personalities were given two minutes to speak about Mr. Gruss. The attraction, however, was the Rav, who was given twenty minutes as the keynote speaker for the evening. The invitation was extended to the Rav against the background of the sharp disappointment that Mr. Gruss had over the Rav's non-compliance with what he thought were the pre-conditions to build the Gruss Center in Jerusalem.

Picking up the Rav that Sunday afternoon (along with my wife, Miriam) to bring him to the Brooklyn dinner, I immediately noticed the tension on his face. The Rav was accompanied by his son-in-law, R' Yitzhak Twersky *zt"l*. Both sat in the backseat of the car and said absolutely nothing along the way. I had an eerie feeling throughout that forty-five minute drive. When we finally arrived at the hall, the Rav's temperament changed in a split second. He was friendly, cordial, and welcomed warmly by … Mr. Gruss himself!

The tensions between the Rav and Mr. Gruss were not top

secret. The Rav, in his opening remarks, wished to dispel the tension immediately. He said that in Biblical Hebrew there are two different words that mean friendship. One is *Re'ah* (רע) and the second is *Yedid* (ידיד). The two are not identical. The first type of friendship is of a temporary nature. Yesterday, he was your friend, but today he could stab you in the back, as the Torah states in Shemot 21:14, וְכִי יָזִד אִישׁ עַל רֵעֵהוּ לְהָרְגוֹ בְעָרְמָה מֵעִם מִזְבְּחִי תִּקָּחֶנּוּ לָמוּת. On the other hand, the friendship of a *Yedid* nature lasts forever, and is capable of surviving the bumps in the relationship. "Joseph Gruss and I are true *Yedidim*," declared the Rav.

The core of the Rav's address that evening focused upon two different types of contributors to the *Mishkan* construction in the desert. Tapping into that week's Torah reading, Vayakhel, he cited the verse (Shemot 35:21) וַיָּבֹאוּ כָּל אִישׁ אֲשֶׁר נְשָׂאוֹ לִבּוֹ וְכֹל אֲשֶׁר נָדְבָה רוּחוֹ showing there were those who contributed with great zeal and enthusiasm, occasionally going beyond the figures originally planned. These emotional givers are characterized as the נשאו לבו. However, there are other contributors who are very calculating in their giving process. They take counsel with their accountants prior to making a pledge. These are the נדבה רוחו type givers. The Rav went on to apply both types of givers as being the hallmark of Joseph Gruss and his philanthropic activities.

> This evening's dinner carried a most interesting postscript. Immediately after the conclusion of the Rav's speech, he motioned to me that we were leaving. To my dismay and that of my wife, as the waiters were rolling out the dinner, the Rav signaled that he wished to leave at that moment. We all left the hall, together with R' Twersky, who asked to be driven back to LaGuardia and make his return flight. We had twenty minutes to accomplish that, and I regretfully informed R' Twersky that it was impossible. He told me that if he makes the flight on time, he will issue me a *Semikha* in *Ma'aseh Merkava* (that angelic chariot of Isaiah 6, and Ezekiel 1-3) as a supernatural driver! He actually did make the flight on

time. Years later, in a visit to the Ben Gurion University as a guest lecturer, he reminded me that he owes me a *Klaf* (a parchment certificate for the "Semikha")!

Meanwhile, at LaGuardia, the Rav decided that he was hungry. As we lived just ten minutes away from the airport in the Kew Gardens Hills neighborhood of Queens, we offered to bring the Rav to our home, feed him, and then return him to his apartment at YU. During this spontaneous three-hour visit, we conversed with the Rav about a variety of topics including the Mussar movement (see Conversation #54) and the status of *Glatt* meat (see Conversation #18). This dinner became one of those lifetime memorable evenings of all times for my wife and me.

45

Soviet Jewry Rallies

The post-Six Day War era in 1967 brought on a euphoric atmosphere amongst Israelis and Diaspora Jews alike. This atmosphere spread to the former Soviet Union where over three million Jews were locked behind the Iron Curtain. Many of these Jews began demanding from the Soviet authorities the right to immigrate to Israel. The leadership of this movement – later to be referred to as "refuseniks" – carried out a heroic struggle against the tyrannical regime in Moscow. Some were given life prison sentences in Siberia.

Public demonstrations against the Soviet Union began to sprout in Israel and throughout the Jewish world. Many YU students became active in the Student Struggle for Soviet Jewry (SSSJ) movement. In the early 1970s, there were two leading Jewish figures who were vehemently opposed to publicly demonstrating against the Soviet authorities (R' Menachem Mendel Schneerson of Lubavitch and R' Pinchas Teitz of Elizabeth, N.J. זכרונם לברכה) – each for his own reason.

The Rav, however, took the position that the Jewish community ought to raise its voice publicly on the matter and show its deep concern for fellow Jews in trouble. R' Aharon Lichtenstein – then the *Rosh Kollel* at YU – released his students for purposes of participating in these demonstrations. Regarding the Rav's attitude on this matter, he once told me that he did not want to be held guilty for the identical sin twice in one lifetime! He was referring to the commandment (Vayikra 19:16) of לא תַעֲמֹד עַל דַּם רֵעֶךָ – not to stand idly by while one's brethren suffer. During the chilling days of the Holocaust, the Rav believed that he, along with the bulk of the American Jewish community, did far too little on behalf of our suffering brethren under Nazi occupation. The Rav felt that he could repent, in a small way, by taking the activist approach to the Soviet Jewish issue.

In a conversation I had in 1983 with Yosef Mendelevitch, a famous "refusenik" from those days, (a conversation carried out while we both did military service together in the Israeli army!), regarding whether or not he was aware, while in solitary confinement in Siberia, of all the demonstrations taking place in the West on his behalf, he noted that he was not absolutely certain that it was the force of the demonstrations which brought down the Soviet government in 1989. However, he did know about the demonstrations going on, and they gave him strength to continue and survive the ordeal for ten years!

The Rav delivering a public address, 1940s.   (*Photo: Alexander Archer*)

IV   Integrity and Sensitivity

It is not sufficient for the Rabbi to know Torah and possess the competence to issue Halakhic decisions. . . . To personify absolute righteousness is the greatest challenge facing the rabbi. The laws of proper behavior between man and his fellow man create the greatest tests that a rabbi must pass. The leading rabbis throughout the generations succeeded magnificently in these areas. They were totally honest in their decisions in monetary litigation. . . . The greatest of rabbis throughout the millennia displayed their greatness in the sphere of social justice.

— *The Rav*, ed. R' Aaron Rakefet-Rothkoff, Vol. 2, 1999,
pp. 47–48

Illustrating the Rav's deep care and sensitivity, a story is told about an episode when the Rav took ill for several weeks and was not present in Shul during those Shabbatot. Upon returning after recuperation from his illness, a long line of well-wishers lined up after the davening to greet the Rav. Each, in his/her own way, inquired about the Rav's health, and each was given a simple, "Fine, thank you" response. At the end of the line, a special needs young girl waited patiently and she, too, asked the Rav very empathetically how he was feeling. To this young girl, the Rav unloaded his whole medical file regarding his condition and various problems. This girl's brother was standing nearby and overheard this entire interchange. Later during the day he saw the Rav and asked him how it was that everybody asked the same question concerning his health, and the Rav simply responded: "Fine, thank you". Yet, his sister had asked him the identical question and the Rav hadn't stopped talking about his medical condition. Why the difference, asked the brother? The Rav very sensitively responded: All these people inquired out of courtesy, so they received a socially polite response. But your sister asked out of deep concern. So, I shared with her what was really happening.

— Reported to me by Bostonian acquaintances

46

The Gruenspecht Family *Shiva* Visit

On a particular Wednesday afternoon at YU, the Rav informed me that he would like to make a *Shiva* visit in the neighborhood of Washington Heights. There didn't seem to me to be any unique features surrounding this *Shiva* visit, as opposed to several other such visits with the Rav. Except that this time, the woman sitting *Shiva* was Susie, daughter of Mr. Eric Gruenspecht *a"h* (and married to my first cousin, Marvin Ammer). I had already paid a family *Shiva* visit earlier during the week. I was quite curious about what the connection was between the Rav and the Gruenspecht family. (I quickly phoned my cousin alerting the family of the Rav's upcoming visit.)

The Rav related to me that approximately thirty years earlier, the Gruenspecht family that was in the meat distributing business, had Yeshiva University's cafeteria as a major client. During those years, new butcheries opened up in the neighborhood carrying "upgraded" Kashrut supervision tags. The competition in the neighborhood was fierce. The easiest way to drag down a competitor was to spread false rumors about them regarding low Kashrut standards.

This situation was brought to the Rav's attention. Knowing the Gruenspecht family, he immediately issued a public statement declaring the Gruenspecht family as God-fearing people who serve the public with impeccable kosher meat products. The Rav told me that not only did his statement salvage the connection with the cafeteria, but it salvaged Gruenspecht's entire business in the neighborhood!

I asked the Rav if he remained in contact with the Gruenspecht family over the past years. He responded negatively. So why the urgency to make this *Shiva* visit, I asked? To which the Rav answered: "So that the family should know that even after thirty years, I haven't changed my mind about the family."

> I was recently informed that not long after the above-described incident, the Rav attended a *Brit* in the Gruenspecht family and insisted that they serve meat at the festive meal.

A situation developed with my own sister, Judy, who was employed as a teacher by a Boro Park Bais Yaakov affiliated school. The teaching staff included many unmarried young ladies looking to advance their careers in education. The salaries offered to the teaching staff were meager, but the opportunity to get started working was worth it all. As it turned out, the school was receiving government funding for these teachers. The teachers were all told to sign the official receipts of the whole amounts. However, as in a classic kickback scam, the teachers had to return to the school approximately two thirds of that sum. The school administration, although willingly committing a felony, felt protected by the fact that a religious person would never be a "*moser*" (someone who would report another Jew to gentile authorities). And, for quite some time, the school was getting away with this scam.

My father *z"l* urged me to hear the Rav out on how to handle this situation. After expressing his absolute disgust that a religious school could be involved in such scandalous behavior, he recommended that my sister threaten to report the school's administration to the Brooklyn's District Attorney to open a criminal investigation. The Rav explained that "*moser*" was a very serious matter in medieval times when "reporting" meant "turning over" (literally: "*moser*") to the authorities. In many cases, an execution would follow. However, in modern times, not reporting to the authorities is an absolute guarantee of perpetuating criminal activity. For sure, this story will go public

at some later date. The public desecration of God's Name (חילול
ה') will ultimately be that much greater. It would be best to nip
it in the bud at some early stage, and suffer the consequences of
a smaller dose of חילול ה', rather than letting it get out of hand.

Furthermore, the demand of the school administrators
for the teachers to sign that they've received their legitimate
compensation, is in itself a serious transgression. A Talmudic
opinion (Ketubot 19a) exists that one should forfeit one's life
rather than sign falsely. (– עדים, שאמרו להם: חתמו שקר ואל תהרגו
יהרגו ואל יחתמו שקר)

Many years later, this particular administrator was caught
in a much more complex criminal situation and was ultimately
sentenced and jailed for his crimes.[1]

1. See R' Hershel Schachter, *Divrei HaRav*, 2010, pp. 2301–231. See also,
R' Aharon Ziegler, *Halakhic Positions of Rabbi Joseph B. Soloveitchik*, Vol.
VII, 2017, p. 29.

48

Operating a Yeshiva without Government Funding

In 1937, the Rav and his wife, Tonya, founded the Maimonides School in the Roxbury neighborhood of Boston (re-located to the Brookline neighborhood in 1962). At the time, all religious and parochial schools had to be independently funded in order to operate. The American doctrine of "separation of Church and State" did not allow for government allocations to such parochial schools. However, by the mid-1970s, political pressures were successfully applied to allow for some sort of government help to these independent school systems. This aid came in the form of lunch programs, textbook purchases, laboratory equipment, and student transportation.

The Rav was confident that as long as he and his wife were at the helm of the institution, there would never be a scandal of misusing government funding. However, as nobody lives forever, the Rav felt that the pressures on subsequent school administrators to balance their budgets would be so heavy, the temptation would always exist to compromise one's integrity vis-à-vis government school allocations. (See Conversation #47 for an excellent example of the Rav's realistic concerns.) Hence, at the Maimonides School, the policy was instituted never to seek out – nor to accept – government allocations for school operations. The school's annual budget would be covered exclusively by tuition payments and voluntary contributions. With this policy, the Rav would guarantee for posterity that no desecration of God's Name (חילול ה') would ever occur due to dishonesty on the public level.

To say that the Rav was to me the most honest and sincere person would be a gross understatement. He was our litmus test and moral compass concerning all issues demanding integrity and honesty. He once told me that to be "*frum*" (scrupulously and devoutly religious) as taught in the first three sections of the *Shulhan Arukh* (אורח חיים, יורה דעה, ואבן העזר) dealing with the ritual dimensions of Torah (Prayer & Blessings, Shabbat & Festivals, Kashrut & Purity, and Marriage & Divorce issues) is a relatively simple matter. However, the more difficult section of Torah to fully observe is that of civil law and interpersonal financial relationships in the fourth order of the *Shulhan Arukh* (חושן משפט).

> In a similar assessment, the Rav's son, R' Prof. Haym Soloveitchik, once stated that some Jews believe in God only with regard to the first three sections of *Shulhan Arukh*. But as to the fourth, dealing with monetary subjects, they become totally pagan!

The Rav's honesty and integrity was painfully tested in the infamous Boston Kashrut scandal of the early 1940s. The Rav was falsely accused of involvement in racketeering schemes and pocketing large sums of money in the process. At the end of the day, the presiding justice on the criminal case, Judge A.K Cohen, not only exonerated the Rav from all charges, but lauded the Rav on his bravery to be principled and stand up for what he thought was right. While scathed somewhat from this horrible incident in his life, the Rav exited with an unparalleled reputation in honesty and integrity.[2]

The Rav once told me that on the printed wrappers of Kosher-supervised food products, the *Hekhsher* (Rabbinic supervision) should include clauses the likes of: "free of any suspicion of theft, tax evasion, and exploitation of workers." These items are no less Torah values than the Kashrut of the food itself.[3]

> It is interesting to note that as of 2005 in Israel, a category of supervision, known as כשרות חברתית (Social Kashrut) was launched by the organization, *Ma'agale Zedek*, spearheaded by Hilli Tropper – today, a Member of Israel's Knesset and Minister of Culture & Sports.

2. See *HaPardes*, (17), 1944, for Judge Cohen's full report and assessment of the Rav's character.

3. See R' Hershel Schachter, *Nefesh HaRav*, 1994, p. 269.

On one bright and early Tuesday morning – a day of picking up the Rav from LaGuardia Airport – I noticed outside my Boro Park window that my car was gone! In a panic, I quickly arranged with my brother to have someone substitute for me. I spent a few hours at the local Police precinct reporting the stolen car. Eventually, I made it to YU, and joined the Rav's *Shiur* in progress. When the Rav saw me enter, he stopped the *Shiur* and offered the blessing (Yerushalmi Berakhot 2:8): המקום ימלא חסרונך (May God restore your loss).

Within twenty-four hours, my car was returned to me, by the police, fully intact. (Who said the Rav wasn't a בעל מופת?)

Bedside Prayer for Dr. Belkin

On *Hol HaMo'ed Pesah*, 1976, the second President of Yeshiva University, Rabbi Dr. Samuel Belkin *z"l*, passed away. Several days earlier, Dr. Belkin lay on his deathbed at the hospital of Einstein's College of Medicine (YU). At that time, a prayer assembly of the entire Yeshiva program of YU, along with its illustrious staff, was held on behalf of the President and *Rosh Yeshiva*. (See Conversation #21.) It was thought that it would be proper for a delegation of the senior Yeshiva staff to officially part with Dr. Belkin in the hospital. After some discussion, it was decided that the "delegation" would consist only of the Rav. For me, this was a very moving experience watching the Rav standing and hovering over an unconscious colleague and friend for thirty years. He said one chapter of the Psalms (in accordance with *Rambam's* directive in *Hilkhot Avel* 14:6), meditated for several minutes in utter silence, and walked out. The Rav was noticeably shaken up by this visit. I recall him telling me something to the effect that if not for Dr. Belkin, there would be no Yeshiva!

How interesting, that after precisely seventeen years to the day (!) on *Hol HaMo'ed Pesah*, the Rav would also depart from this world. (See Conversation #70.)

Several weeks after that Pesah, a graveside *Shloshim* memorial service was held for Dr. Belkin z"l in the presence of the entire RIETS faculty and student body. The Rav, at the time, strongly recommended that the entire service – including eulogies

– be led by students only. While there was some discussion on the subject, the Rav's desires ultimately prevailed. The YU administration arranged for limousine service for the senior rabbinic staff. The Rav, however, declined this gesture, and told the Acting President, R' Miller, that he'll be going with Adler! In my car that afternoon with the Rav were my two brothers, R' Yosef and Donny. For my younger brother, Donny, this was a unique – and only – opportunity he would have to enjoy a one-on-one talk with the Rav.

On the subject of prayer in times of peril and moments of crisis, I had the following conversation with the Rav relating to the Talmudic dispute over whether or not the evening prayer – *Ma'ariv* – is an obligatory prayer no different from the morning *Shaharit* or the afternoon *Minha* prayers.[4] The Halakha is in accordance with the view that *Ma'ariv* is an optional (רשות) prayer. In practice, however, all Jewish communities have adopted the custom of viewing *Ma'ariv* as an obligatory (חובה) prayer.[5]

The Talmud (*Berakhot* 26b) cites the tradition of our forefathers, Abraham, Isaac, and Jacob, having initiated the three time frameworks for daily prayer. Abraham initiated the morning *Shaharit*; Isaac continued with the afternoon *Minha*; and Jacob prayed the *Ma'ariv* nighttime prayer.[6] The question that I posed to the Rav was why Jacob was accredited with initiating the prayer, *Ma'ariv*, a prayer that would be Halakhically classified as "optional" (רשות) status?

With the Rav's permission I proceeded to suggest that the evening *Ma'ariv* prayer is far from being an "optional" prayer in relation to the others. The absolute necessity of composing

---

4. See *Berakhot* 27b, תפלת ערבית, רבן גמליאל אומר: חובה, רבי יהושע אומר: רשות. אמר אביי: הלכה כדברי האומר חובה. ורבא אמר: הלכה כדברי האומר רשות.

5. See Rambam, *Hilkhot Tefillah* 1:6, ואף ע"פ כן נהגו כל ישראל בכל מקומות מושבותיהם להתפלל ערבית וקבלוה עליהם כתפלת חובה.

6. See Rambam, *Hilkhot Melakhim* 9:1.

liturgical texts for all, by Men of the Great Assembly (אנשי כנסת הגדולה), came at a price of spontaneity in prayer. Our Sages were keenly aware of the fact that statutory ritual prayer carries with it the rigid adherence to exact texts. This was of great concern to our Sages.[7] During the nighttime, symbolizing confusion, distress and peril, our prayer could revert back to its more pristine form lacking absolute formality, thus allowing for some measure of flexibility in our prayer performance. To this end, the Mishnah (Berakhot 4:1) states: תפילת הערב אין לה קבע – the evening prayer lacks exactness and precision in terms of its time framework and allows for some measure of spontaneous prayer. This loose formulation is directly associated with the Halakhic view that the *Ma'ariv* prayer is "optional" (Berakhot 27b). Hence, it was the greatness of our forefather, Jacob, for having paved the way for the maintenance of some degree of spontaneous prayer within the framework of daily standardized prayer.

I was humbled by the Rav's endorsement of this homiletical approach.

7. See Mishnah, Avot 2:13, אל תעש תפלתך קבע אלא רחמים ותחנונים לפני המקום. ברוך הוא

52 Blessings Received from an Ordinary Person

The Talmud (Berakhot 7a) relates that one should not take lightly a blessing received from even an ordinary person – לא תהא ברכת הדיוט קלה בעיניך.

In discussing this with the Rav, I mentioned that while I have no idea exactly how blessings of a *zaddik* function in bringing about desired results, at least there, we have a concept of צדיק גוזר והקב"ה מקיים (based upon *Mo'ed Katan* 16b). The idea is that one can tap into the merits of the *zaddik*, which, in turn, will work in one's favor when requesting help from God.

However, it wasn't clear at all how the blessings of an ordinary person can have any impact on one's life. The Rav explained to me a fundamental concept in life: sixty percent of success in all of life's endeavors – health, financial, and social – can be attributed to the person's will to succeed. The problem is that life is an obstacle course making the realization of one's success that much more difficult. When another person greets someone with wishes for good health, for example, it removes one of those obstacles in life's erratic pathways. The person's will to succeed thereby becomes strengthened and fortified, giving him that much better a chance to achieve the desired results.

In the early 1970s, the Rav was no longer in his prime physically. But, he still had much energy and enthusiasm to continue teaching Torah. Occasionally, the Rav would give expression to the awareness of his aging. He spoke not of fearing death, but rather of fearing the loss of his intellectual capabilities. The Rav's New York teaching schedule included the weekly Tuesday evening *Shiur* at Manhattan's midtown Synagogue, Congregation Moriah. This two-hour *Shiur* drew a regular attendance of nearly three hundred participants. The problem was that this Synagogue occupied a building where one had to walk up two flights of stairs to enter the sanctuary. In the mid-1970s, this walkup became a serious struggle for the Rav. I offered my suggestion to the Rav that perhaps the time had come to permanently give up this *Shiur*. To which the Rav sharply retorted: "You mean to throw in the towel to the *Mal'akh HaMavet* (Angel of Death)?" "Never"(!!!), he yelled in frustration. It was painfully obvious that he was planning to continue the *Shiur*. With time, reality ran its course, and the Rav found it impossible to walk up the two flights of stairs. The *Shiur* was temporarily re-located in the neighborhood to the Young Israel of the West Side for several weeks until his pains subsided and was, once again, able to walk the steps at Moriah. Upon his return to the original location, the Rav spoke of his feelings in the temporary location in terms of limited exile

The Rav and the Lubavitcher Rebbe, 1980, OU Jewish Action.
(*Photo: Jewish Educational Media*)

that atones – a thought borne out by the very Talmudic section under discussion at that time.[8]

> I must confess that during the 2020 coronavirus pandemic this sensation of "limited exile", described by the Rav, overcame me as well, having been forced to leave the confines of our hospitable synagogues for makeshift outdoor street and backyard prayer gatherings.

In general, the Rav objected to taking painkillers to alleviate his suffering, because he felt that this type of medication could negatively impact his cognitive abilities. The Rav was not prepared to forfeit the latter in order to relieve pain. He actually told me of the great pleasure he had tearing up a painkiller prescription in front of his physician!

8. Tractate *Ta'anit* 16a. See R' Hershel Schachter, *Divrei HaRav*, 2010, pp. 231–232.

V   Personal Conduct and Relationships

Man must not always be victor. From time to time triumph should turn into defeat. Man, in Judasim, was created for both victory and defeat – he is both king and saint. He must know how to fight for victory and also how to suffer defeat. Modern man is frustrated and perplexed because he cannot take defeat. He is simply incapable of retreating humbly. Modern man boasts quite often that he has never lost a war. He forgets that defeat is built into the very structure of victory, that there is, in fact, no total victory; man is finite, so is his victory. Whatever is finite is imperfect; so is man's triumph.

– R' Joseph B. Soloveitchik, "Majesty and Humility,"
Tradition (17:2), 1978, p. 36

You could hardly imagine that he [the Rav] was among the humblest of men.... There were countless times and situations which surely illustrated for me this humility. Over and over again, I was amazed by his "anavah," which was so natural that it could almost be missed. Humility too obvious may not be humility.

– R' Zevulun Charlop, "Wherever You Find His Greatness, There You Will Find His Humility," *Memories of a Giant*, 2003, pp. 151–152

54   The Hassidic and the Mussar Movements

During the nineteenth century, Eastern European Jewry could be divided into two basic camps: the *Hassidim* and their staunch opponents, the *Mitnagdim*. Geographically, Poland was more of a Hassidic center, while Lithuania was home to the opponents of Hassidic thought. Within the Lithuanian Yeshiva world, there, too, fragmentation existed between the advocates of the Mussar movement (founded by R' Yisrael Salanter *zt"l*) and the opponents to this type of character-building education.

The Soloveitchik family, spiritual heirs to the Gaon of Vilna's fierce opposition to the Hassidic movement, clearly stood with the *Mitnagdim*. Yet, the Rav, for sure not a Hassid, had an affinity for the Hassidic movement – especially for Habad. (In a 1954 letter to a Habad Rabbi, the Rav wrote: "A touch of Hassidut is hidden in me" – נימה של חסידות גנוזה בי).[1] Perhaps this was a result of three generation's worth of personal relationships with the Rebbes of Habad, including that of the Rav and the last Rebbe, R' Menachem Mendel Schneerson *zt"l*. (See Conversations #57 and #58.). The Rav spoke privately of an unpublished commentary that he authored on the book of Tanya. (See Conversation #28.) In his public addresses, it was not infrequent for the Rav to quote and analyze ideas from the Tanya. He actually once stated publicly that if forced to become a Hassid, he would choose Habad! On one occasion, speaking about וידוי (confession) in the *Yom Kippur* liturgy, the Rav

---

1. R' Hershel Schachter, *Mipnenei HaRav*, 2001, p. 187.

spoke warmly of his experience in Warsaw during his youth, praying with *Hassidim* of *Ger*. R' Hershel Schachter[2] reports that in the Rav's Berlin days he often frequented the *Shteibel* of the Dombrover Rebbe.[3]

On the other hand, in the *Mitnagdim* world, the Rav never identified with the Mussar movement. He did not believe that character building should take place listening to public discourses or by reading material. In his mind, excellence in character can only be achieved by having a human role model who will silently project the desirable traits for others to emulate. The Rav told me that the Hassidic movement was a tremendous success while the Mussar movement was a dismal failure. The reasons for this are that Hassidic thought spoke to the average person and elevated him spiritually, whereas the Mussar movement preached to the elite only (not a popular position), or taught about the low value and esteem of human existence.

> The Rav once quipped ironically that upon "graduation" from Kelm (a leading center of the Mussar movement), the students were given a badge proudly announcing that they have achieved humility ("I am an עניו")!
>
> In a private visit to my home in Queens, N.Y., (see Conversation #44, end) the Rav, scanning the few books I had on the shelves at the time, took note of R' Eliyahu Dessler's מכתב מאליהו, and asked me: "Who here reads Rav Dessler"? I responded that they were my wife's books! To which the Rav continued to probe: "Is she related to him"? Since then we've called him: "Uncle Dessler."

2. Ibid., p. 61.

3. A fascinating anecdote was provided by the Rav himself reflecting upon his experiences at the *Modzitzer Shteibel* as a youngster. See, Arnold Lustiger, *Before Hashem You Shall Be Purified*, 1998, pp. 37–38.

55   A Humble Disposition

The book title, *Majesty and Humility*, 2012, (R' Reuven Ziegler's excellent work on the Rav's thoughts) describes the Rav's personality accurately. His stature was nothing less than royal and majestic in the spirit of מאן מלכי – רבנן. On the other hand, the Rav maintained a humble disposition. Humility, to the Rav, had nothing to do with a sense of worthlessness. He believed that true humility (ענוה) was a function of an accurate self-evaluation – not greater and not lower. The Torah (Bamidbar 12:3) speaks of Moses as: וְהָאִישׁ מֹשֶׁה עָנָיו מְאֹד מִכֹּל הָאָדָם אֲשֶׁר עַל פְּנֵי הָאֲדָמָה ("And Moses the man was more humble than any human being on earth"). Moses did not see himself as worthless at all. He had a correct evaluation of himself, knowing fully well that he was Moses our Teacher! So, too, did R' Akiva know who R' Akiva was; the *Rambam* knew who the *Rambam* was; and the Rav said about himself (!), "and I know exactly who I am."

> The Rav once told my brother, R' Yosef Adler, that in the town of his childhood, Khaslovici, he would write *Bar Mitzvah* talks for the thirteen-year-old boys on the basis of the שאגת אריה (the eighteenth century Halakhic work known as the litmus test for Torah scholars) – a book that the Rav himself completed studying at age ten!

This was all said by the Rav in the context of resolving the perplexing issue concerning *Rambam's* statement prohibiting permanent residence in Egypt,[4] and the fact that he himself spend most of his adult life on Egyptian soil. The Rav explained that during his short sojourn in Eretz Yisrael, Rambam decided that his presence was vitally necessary in Egypt to thwart off the spiritually dangerous Karaite adherents. He would direct his talents and efforts in Egypt, despite the three Biblical prohibitions involved, in order to spiritually rescue the large Egyptian Jewish community. (עת לעשות לה' – הפרו תורתך) The Rav concluded by saying that people should realize that he, too, had a responsibility to the rescue of American Orthodoxy at the expense of *Aliya* to Israel.

> I once asked the Rav's daughter, Dr. Tova Lichtenstein, about how Israel would look today, had the Rav accepted the Chief Rabbi position in 1960. (See Conversation #40.) Her immediate response was: "And how would American Jewry look today had the Rav left the scene in 1960?!"
>
> (Dr. Tova Lichtenstein made a similar comment after posing the question, "And if the Rav would have won the 1935 Tel Aviv Chief Rabbi position," in *Rav B'Olam HeHadash*, 2010, p. 535.)

4. *Hilkhot Melachim* 5:7.

56 — The Two Hayims of the 19th Century

The Rav once shared with me his view that in the nineteenth century, the two most outstanding Torah luminaries (גדולים) were the "Two Hayims" – his grandfather, R' Hayim Soloveitchik *zt"l* and (to my great surprise) the Rebbe of Zanz, R' Hayim Halberstam *zt"l*. To me, it was no surprise at all that the Rav's grandfather was on this list. But, I was taken aback by the second name – the founder of the Zanz Hassidic dynasty. The Rav felt that in Lithuanian Yeshiva circles, there was an overall lack of appreciation for the Torah scholars of Galicia. The Rav believed that the Responsa of the Rebbe of Zanz, the *Divrei Hayim*, were masterpieces of Torah.

The Rav also valued seriously another Galician scholar, R' Yosef Babad *zt"l* of Tarnopol, the author of the *Minhat Hinukh* – one of the only *Halakhic* works that he actually completed during his formative years under the tutelage of his father, R' Moshe Soloveitchik *zt"l*.[5]

5. See also, R' Hershel Schachter, *Mipnenei HaRav*, 2001, p. 163.

57   The Rav and the Rebbe in Berlin

In 1926, the Rav left his parental home in Warsaw and set out to study philosophy at the University of Berlin. He would spend seven years there earning his doctoral degree by 1932 – the year of his migration to the United States.[6]

At the university, the Rav was told that a highly introverted student in the department was none other than R' Menachem Mendel Schneerson *zt"l* – the son-in-law of the sixth Lubavitcher Rebbe. The Rav befriended this student – a friendship that would last a lifetime. (See Conversation #58.) The Rav reminisced that the Rebbe would sit in the lecture hall with holy books – Halakhic and Kabbalistic works – in a vertical position, somewhat imitating a Sepharadi Torah read in the Synagogue. It appeared as if his head was totally immersed in his holy studies and not really paying attention to the lecture at all. However, when it came to the end of semester grades, R' Menachem Mendel Schneerson received the highest grades of his fellow classmates. It was clear to the Rav that the future Rebbe's head functioned simultaneously on two frequencies. As he was deeply engrossed in his Torah studies, he would also be able to concentrate on the academic philosophical lecture.

At that time, another future Torah giant, R' Yitzhak Hutner *zt"l*, attended the philosophy courses at the University of Berlin. The Rav retrospectively commented that with the three of them in the lecture hall, "רחמנות (compassion) on the lecturers!"

---

6. See R. Hershel Schachter, *Mipnenei HaRav*, 2001, pp. 166–167.

A facinating anecdote was related to me by R' Menachem Genack. On one Purim day in Berlin, R' Menachem Mendel Schneerson was intoxicated with wine to the extent that while walking in a park he was acting in a way that prompted his arrest by the local police. Upon hearing of this arrest, the Rav went to the police station personally to bail out his friend – the future Lubavitcher Rebbe. Knowing the history of Habad, of previous Rebbes having been incarcerated in Russian jails and subsequently freed (which generated several Lubavitch festivals), the Rav quipped to the Rebbe that now that he has been jailed and freed – he is certainly fit to become the next Lubavicher Rebbe![7]

7. In his book, Rebbe, 2014, p. 303 (photo caption), R' Joseph Telushkin reports that the Rebbe responded to a comment that he and the Rav "were good friends (in Berlin)," by saying: "Much more than is known." For a general overview of the Rav and Habad, see R' Aharon Rakefet's article, "The Rebbe and the Rav," in the Orthodox Union's *Jewish Action*, (summer), 2014.

On 10 Shevat 5740 (1980), R' Menachem Mendel Schneerson *zt"l* celebrated his thirtieth year as Rebbe of Lubavitch (Habad). As a gesture of honor and friendship, the Rav decided to attend the Rebbe's huge get-together (*fahrbrengen*) that evening. The plan was for the Rav to enter at the time the Rebbe would be entering the hall. He was to stay approximately twenty minutes (of a six-hour get-together). In fact, the Rav stayed for over two hours!

As the Rav rose to part with the Rebbe, the Rebbe jumped up to properly take leave of the Rav. After moments of smiles and warm handshakes, the Rav left the hall en route back to his YU apartment.

At the time, I was already an Israeli immigrant, reading about this event in the next morning's newspapers. It was reported that at the moment of parting, the Rebbe told the Rav that he represents seven generations from R' Sheneur Zalman of Liadi – the founder of the Habad movement and the author of "the Tanya," and that the Rav was seven generations (albeit not genealogically) from R' Eliyahu – the Gaon of Vilna. Never to be forgotten was the schism between the Hassidic movement and the Mitnagdim as represented by the excommunication edict issued by the Gaon of Vilna against the founding Rebbe of Habad. However, continued the Rebbe, let this great assembly witness the mutual love, friendship, and respect the two had for each other (באהבה ואחוה ושלום ורעות). Apparently, said the Rebbe, the souls of the Gaon of Vilna and the author of the Tanya made peace with each other in the heavenly world.

I read all of this in the Israeli press. I knew that I would have to receive confirmation of the details of this episode. Several months later, in June, 1980, upon my first return visit to the United States after my *Aliya* to Israel, I paid the Rav a visit. At the time, I questioned the Rav about this episode in the Rebbe's residence, 770 Eastern Parkway in Crown Heights, Brooklyn, NY. I asked the Rav what he thought about the Rebbe's comment of the Gaon of Vilna and the author of the Tanya making up in the heavenly world. The Rav immediately responded that he fully agreed that the two had finally made peace with each other. However, this did not take place in 770, but rather in Auschwitz, Bergen Belsen, Maydanek, Dachau, and in all the many other camps during the Holocaust. No distinction was made in the extermination process between *Hassidim* and *Mitnagdim*. The Rav then added that my generation's awareness of the *Hassidim/Mitnagdim* schism is reduced to outer garb only. We don't have a clue about how the schism impacted upon the different brands of "service of God." How tragic it is that only in the aftermath of the Holocaust would an era of reconciliation begin between these two groups.[8]

As an appendix to the story of the Rav's 770 visit in 1980, I recall that after I had taken the Rav, in 1975, to the Brooklyn cemetery gravesite of his father, R' Moshe, on his *Yahrzeit* (see Conversation #11), I realized that we were no more than ten minutes away from 770. I asked the Rav if he would be interested in dropping in at the Rebbe completely unannounced. He actually gave it some thought – ten minutes worth (!) – but then opted to return to his apartment at YU.

8. A slightly different version of this event, along with the Rav's comments, were summarized, by R' Hershel Schachter from hearsay in his *Mipnenei HaRav*, 2001, p. 187.
A fifteen-minute YouTube clip of the Rav and Rebbe at this event (annotated by the late R' Herschel Schacter *z"l* – the US Army Chaplain at the liberation of the Buchenwald concentration camp) can be viewed by searching for "Rav" and "Rebbe."

In 1975, I reported to the Rav about the talk delivered the previous evening by the Lubavitcher Rebbe. The Rav showed great interest in the content of the talk. Among other things, the Rebbe, at that time, launched his new project of having all young girls above the age of three light Shabbat candles at home. The Rebbe, on a Kabbalistic note, described the spiritual upgrade in one's home by having additional Shabbat candles burn. (See Conversation #15.) He also felt that this would be a successful educational tool to educate the otherwise uninitiated young women in Jewish practices. Most interesting to the Rav, however, was the Rebbe's argument on Halakhic grounds that this project was tenable and not to be considered a deviation from general Jewish custom. The Rebbe crossed *Hassidim/ Mitnagdim* lines by citing the home of R' Hayim Soloveitchik of Brisk where the daughters lit Shabbat candles regularly from after the *Bat Mitzvah* age of twelve. Although age twelve is not age three, nevertheless in both cases it is prior to the young woman's marriage. The Rav, indeed, confirmed to me that the custom of his family was to have the daughters light Shabbat candles at age twelve – a custom maintained until this very day by his offspring.[9]

The Rebbe went on to provide somewhat of a proof text to lend backing to the project by citing the words of *Rashi* to Bereishit 24:67, which speak about Rebbeca's entering into

---

9. See R' Hershel Schachter, *Mipnenei HaRav*, 2001, p. 62.

Isaac's tent and the return of all that was lost after the death of
Sarah. Among other things, *Rashi* notes: היה נר דלוק מערב שבת לערב
שבת. The Rebbe, in adopting Rashi's point of view that Rebbeca
was three years old at that time, allowed him to conclude that
even a three-year-old may light the Shabbat candles. To this the
Rav quipped: "I fully agree that if a three- year-old girl gets
married, she should light Shabbat candles!"

Many years later, this conversation of mine with the Rav
made its way to Kfar Habad in Israel, and they sent me a printed
transcript (in Yiddish) of the Rebbe's talk from 1975. There, the
Rebbe specifically pointed out that the *Midrash*, upon which
Rashi based himself, was on the first half of the same verse
which reports Rebbeca's marriage to Isaac. Hence, this Midrash
can serve as a source for his newly-announced project.

In 1974, I took note of a Yiddish newspaper item reporting that several years earlier the Rav had conducted private conversations on theology with the Catholic Church's Dutch Cardinal Johannes Willebrands. I asked the Rav, if the report was true (it, indeed, transpired on March 8th, 1971), how does that behavior accord with the Rav's celebrated position in his *Tradition*, 1964, article, "Confrontation," where he takes a strong stand against dialogue with the Church, at the same time vehemently recommending against participation in the Pope's Ecumenical Council?[10] The Rav responded that in his article he addressed the issue of public policy. Aside from all the arguments voiced in the article, the Rav confided in me that in order to dialogue with the Church, one had to be an expert in Christianity (as in the case of Ramban's thirteenth century disputations). He then said: "how many serious Torah spokesman of today are familiar with Christianity as much as I am!"

Thus, on a private level, the Rav felt that there was something to be gained by having communication lines open and available for the Jewish people. He felt an obligation to have a relationship with the local Church leadership.

It is interesting to note that in an October 28th, 1985 address in Rome to the International Catholic/Jewish Liason Committee, Cardinal Willebrands referred to his conversation with the Rav by stating: "And I recall vividly in this connection

10. See R' Hershel Schachter, *Divrei HaRav*, 2010, pp. 194–197.

a conversation I had in a New York hotel March 8, 1971, with Rabbi Joseph Soloveitchik, the venerable Jewish teacher of so many generations of rabbis and, at least indirectly, of very many Jews at large. After having said what I just repeated, only in a more beautiful and moving way, he went on to say that in any case 'all dialogue between Jews and Christians cannot but be religious and theological because', he continued, 'you are a priest and I am a rabbi; can we speak otherwise than at the level of religion? Our culture is certainly a religious one.'"[11]

11. For an analytical view of the Rav's general attitude towards Jewish/Christian polemics and its relevance today, see R. Shlomo Riskin, "Rav Soloveitchik and the Jewish/Christian Dialogue" (Hebrew), *Emunot V'De'ot B'Mishnat HaRav Yosef Dov Soloveitchik*, 2001, pp. 77–97.

For a comprehensive overview of the Rav's position many years after the appearance of "Confrontation," see Boston College, *Rabbi Joseph Soloveitchik on Interreligious Dialogue: Forty Years Later*, 2003, at the Boston College website: *https://www.bc.edu/content/dam/files/research_sites/cjl/texts/center/conferences/soloveitchik/*

After my engagement to Miriam Halberstadt in the winter of 1975, my *Kallah* and I discussed various family customs. The Halberstadt family hailed from Frankfurt, Germany, and kept many of the long-standing customs of the *"yekkes."* (The Rav heard, "Halberstam," and wanted to know ironically if the *Kallah* is a *Sanzer.*) One of the more popular of these customs was the reduced waiting time from six to three hours between eating meat and milk.[12] The Adler side, however, came from Galicia, Poland where six hours became the norm after the sixteenth century. The problem was that my grandfather, Gershon Adler *a"h*, migrated to Berlin between the world wars. Many of the (convenient) local customs were adopted by many Polish migrants to Germany, including the custom of waiting only three hours after eating meat. My father *z"l* was born into that situation, and carried it into our home in New York. I remember waiting only three hours after meat before eating milk. Miriam suggested that I consult the Rav as to whether or not I have an obligation to return to the Galician custom – my original family heritage – and upgrade to waiting six hours.

The Rav said that I have no obligation to return to the stricter six-hour view, but can continue with the more lenient three-hour view to which I was conditioned at home. When I asked whether it would be preferable to upgrade to the stricter opinion, the Rav quipped: "Are you looking for a *Humrah* (strict

12. See Prof. Daniel Sperber, *Minhag Yisrael*, Vol. 1, 1989, p. 45, note 18.

opinion)? I can only tell you that there are two areas where the *Humrah* approach is highly advisable." The Rav then elaborated on the transgression of engaging in slanderous talk (לשון הרע) and the Biblical commandment to give charity (צדקה). (See Conversation #66.) One should be particularly strict in these two areas throughout one's lifetime. In other areas of Torah, it would be okay to take the lenient path!

Wedding Gift and Advice

An excellent example of the Rav's character as a מכיר טוב (showing appreciation for all the rides and personal care), the Rav, who could not make the special trip to New York for my wedding during the summer months, nevertheless felt that a very generous wedding gift was in order. (As a sentimental gesture, I first copied the check for posterity and then deposited it in the bank!). I'll never forget his advice to me on the very first day of Yeshiva in September, 1975: "Keep her happy!" Indespensible wise words, indeed!

63   No Laziness on the Rabbinic Watch

The Rav once told me that he received a call from a man in Boston with a question regarding an *eiruv* that he constructed in his private yard for purposes of carrying on Shabbat to/from his outdoor Sukkah. (In spite of the Rav's overall objections to mounting a citywide *eiruv*, he had no difficulty with such construction on private grounds.) The details, however, of this particular *eiruv* were somewhat elaborate and unclear. The Rav had a difficult time, over the phone, to fully grasp the onsite situation. He then boarded the trolley for over an hour's journey to this fellow's home, took one peek at the *eiruv* construction, and ruled immediately that it satisfied the Halakhic specifications. He explained to the man why it was okay, and then returned home on the trolley for over another hour. I asked the Rav: why was he telling this to me? To this he responded: I know that one day you are going to become a Shul Rabbi. Don't ever be lazy on the rabbinic watch! And, always maximize the opportunity of a *She'eilah* (Halakhic inquiry) to teach someone Torah.

I've personally adopted this credo during my thirty-six years of service in the rabbinate in various stations.

64 Entering the Rabbinate

During the winter of 1977, I was appointed to my first rabbinical position at Congregation Sons of Israel in Long Island City, N.Y. At the time, I was still in my final stages of the *Semikha* (ordination) program at YU. The community was willing to gamble that I would successfully complete the *Semikha* program by that summer.

In line with the Talmudic directive (Sanhedrin 5b) that a student should not render a Halakhic decision without prior permission from his teacher (תלמיד אל יורה אלא אם כן נוטל רשות מרבו), I sought the Rav's permission to accept this position. The Rav was extremely encouraging. He felt that not having to relocate "out of town" (a New Yorker phrase meaning anywhere in the United States outside of New York City) was already an excellent beginning. Although Sons of Israel was a modest Synagogue, he predicted that with time I would find myself in one of the larger New York Synagogues.

The Rav brought me back to the scene of his father, R' Moshe, receiving a blessing from his father, R' Hayim, as he assumed the rabbinate in the town of Khaslovici. R' Hayim told his son to remember the dictum in the opening Mishnah of Avot 1:1, הוו מתונים בדין (be patient in judgement). The Rav explained to me that this means that a Rabbi should not make a federal case out of every Synagogue/community issue. He should carefully choose his battles, and only take up the battle when an absolutely critical issue is at stake. Failure to adopt this sound advice would spell early doom for the Rabbi in his position.

The Rav illustrated this point quite clearly from his failure in 1932 on his first rabbinic watch in Boston. That year, *Rosh Hashanah* fell out on Shabbat (October 1st). At the Musaf service, the Rav noticed that the *kohanim* were not ascending to perform the priestly blessings (ברכת כהנים). He asked the Synagogue President why the *kohanim* were not in position to perform their religious duty. The response was that in the history of this Synagogue, the custom was that on Shabbat the priestly blessings were never performed. The Rav believed that this was incorrect, and that the *kohanim* should perform their religious task. A serious argument developed which ended by having the Rav leave the position by *Yom Kippur* just ten days later! The Rav continued by telling me that he was right; and that he was so wrong! It wasn't worth giving up the position over this issue.[13]

Another piece of sage advice from the Rav was the idea that a community Rabbi is not exempt from two vital commandments: Torah study and giving charity (צדקה). Furthermore, the Rav strongly advised me that in all fund-raising events, I should match the highest donor of the community! This is the only method of educating the congregants to be generous in charity. And I would have nothing to lose by adopting this policy, for our Sages (*Ta'anit* 9a) have assured us that regular charity is the pathway to wealth (עשר תעשר – עשר בשביל שתתעשר). (See Conversation #66 for an elaboration of the Rav and charity.)

On another occasion, the Rav suggested to me that the combination of one's Semikha, along with the official congregational appointment (מינוי) as its community Rabbi, allows for the Divinely-inspired guiding spirit (סייעתא דשמיא) to hover over the Rabbi's Halakhic and communal guidance abilities. (See Conversation #1.)

In general, the Rav reminded me of his grandfather, R' Hayim's priority in the rabbinate – to help people in need. On his tombstone in Warsaw, it reads: רב חסד. The Rav blessed me that this should be my motto in my future rabbinic life.[14]

---

13. See R' Hershel Schachter, *Nefesh HaRav*, 1994, p. 132.
14. See R' Hershel Schachter, *Mipnenei HaRav*, 2001, p. 182.

65

Every practicing community Rabbi knows that there are occasions when he is called upon to eulogize an individual with whom he never had any contact. I asked the Rav if he could offer some practical pointers on how to go about preparing such a eulogy. The Rav responded that, in all honesty, he never eulogized anyone whom he didn't know personally. So, he would not be a helpful source of good advice.

However, the Rav added that when you do eulogize an individual with whom you were acquainted, you are permitted an inflation rate of no more than 10% in describing the individual's personality. One must present a reasonable presentation of the person's life and not fall into the trap of saying what the mourners would like him to say. (These sentiments were said to me returning from a funeral with the Rav where one of the eulogizers exaggerated beyond reasonable proportions in portraying the deceased person.)

In general, the Rav told me that he preferred to deliver a eulogy at the *Shloshim* (end of the thirty-day period of mourning), for at that time, he would have sufficient time to organize his thoughts and think clearly about the person being eulogized. Such a eulogy far surpassed a half-baked talk at the funeral itself.

66   Charity and Philanthropic Activities

Three particularly important character traits – all within the area of interpersonal relationships – were the hallmark of the Rav's behavior. They include הכרת הטוב (showing appreciation – see Conversation #62), כבוד הבריות (protecting human dignity), and צדקה (charity and philanthropy – see Conversation #64).

It is not well-known that aside from his unusual greatness as a Talmudist, a teacher, a philosopher and a speaker, the Rav was an astonishingly outstanding בעל צדקה (philanthropist) as well. This does not mean that when everyone was putting nickels and dimes into the charity boxes, the Rav would put in a quarter. It means that he was ready and willing to share substantial sums of money with a variety of personal and communal causes.

A reliable and very loyal-to-the-Rav Bostonian told me that in earlier years several dedicated friends of the Rav, who were particularly gifted in the financial investment world, suggested to the Rav that he invest his meager savings. This suggestion netted the Rav a fortune in seven digits. At the time it was reported that the Rav was donating 60% of his holdings and earnings to charitable causes! These causes included maintaining the financial health of families in need, along with communal/institutional support. He, of course, supported his own cherished Maimonides School in Boston. It was also reported that in the 1960s he was sending $10,000 a year to his Soloveitchik cousins in Jerusalem to support the Brisker Yeshiva of his uncle, R' Velvele. (Bear in mind that in 1964 one could purchase an apartment in the upper-class neighborhood of Rehavia in Jerusalem for $42,000.) And this, despite the fact that his cousins ostracized him for committing the two most serious "crimes" – attending the university and becoming a Mizrahi Religious Zionist.

In a risky act of hutzpah, I asked the Rav if there was any truth to his giving 60% of his monies to charity. While the Halakha allows one to go beyond the 10% obligation in charity, the Talmud (*Ketubot* 50a) does speak of an upper limit of 20% and no more (אל יבזבז יותר מחומש).

The Rav could have opted to ignore my question, or perhaps responded very bluntly that this was none of my concern. However, he chose to respond with his sense of humor by saying that I obviously had forgotten a verse in *Kohelet* 7:20, כִּי אָדָם אֵין צַדִּיק בָּאָרֶץ אֲשֶׁר יַעֲשֶׂה טּוֹב וְלֹא יֶחֱטָא ("There is no righteous person who has not even one sin"). The Rav added: "And I didn't want to make *Shlomo HaMelekh* into a liar!" He then said that after one hundred and twenty years, he will stand before the Divine throne and the charge will be read about this terrible sin of overspending on charity. The Rav said he will break out with a big smile and declare: "Guilty as charged!" Several moments afterwards, the Rav explained that in his situation, he had minimal financial expenses. He, therefore, saw himself as an agent of God to help others in need. That was his financial blessing. (Many years later, the 60% figure was confirmed to me by a member of the Rav's family.)

Illustrating the Rav's overly generous nature in philanthropy, the following anecdote is told about a collector from a Jerusalem-based orphanage, sponsored by the extremist Neturei Karta (anti-Zionist) movement, arriving in Boston to fund-raise. He went to see an important community leader, Mr. Abe Levovitz *a"h*, who gave him a check of a certain amount. Later that day, Mr. Levovitz was on his way to see the Rav on some community matter, when out the door came this collector who told Mr. Levovitz that he should be ashamed of himself, because R' Soloveitchik gave him a check much larger than he did! Mr. Levovitz entered the Rav's apartment and told the Rav: Do you know who this man is? Should you visit Israel one day, he will arrange a demonstration at the Israeli airport with large posters reading: "Rabbi Soloveitchik – Go Home!" The Rav calmed down Mr. Levovitz by telling him: Yes, I know exactly who he is. But, he assured me that he won't use the charity money that I gave him to finance posters for the demonstration![15]

Another such story, related by R' Azarya Berzon – The Rav's Thursday afternoon driver form YU back to LaGuardia Airport during the mid 1970s – (printed in the Orthodox Union's weekly *Torah Tidbits, Pesah/Shabbat Hagdol* issue, 2020), goes as follows:

On a bus trip from Boston to New York, I met two students from the Lakewood Yeshiva. To start a conversation I asked them, "What brought you to Boston?" They told me that they volunteered to go on a fundraising trip between school terms. When I asked them, "How did it go?" they responded, "Not too well, except for one nice check that we received".... They began telling me that they went to the Twersky home to see the Rav. Rabbi Twersky *zt"l* answered the door and told them that the Rav was resting and that he couldn't be disturbed. But as they were leaving, a voice from upstairs called, "Who's there?" Rabbi Twersky answered, "Two students from Lakewood Yeshiva." The Rav said, "Let them stay!" He came downstairs to ask how his friend Rabbi Shneur Kotler was doing. The *Talmidim* left the house with the best check they picked up in in the city of Boston.[16]

> On the subject of the Rav's financial wealth, I once dealt with a situation where a check that the Rav wrote bounced back from the bank. The Rav was bewildered, knowing fully well that there was coverage for this check in his Boston account. He asked

15. This story is reported by Mr. Levovitz himself in "The Rav's Human Qualities Evoke Indelible Memories," Memories of a Giant, 2003, p. 233.

16. Several of these anecdotes were incorporated by R' Menachem Kasdan, in his *Yesodei HaTzdedakah*, 2009, p. 584.

me to phone the bank president (!) for him. The Rav took the phone and asked what his balance was. I noticed his eyes rolling when the he heard the figures. He hung up and told me to call up Mayor Beame (the mayor of New York City, then in the midst of a municipal bankruptcy situation) and tell him the he is prepared to bail out the city!!!

67   The Yeshiva University Cafeteria

It was a rare event, but occasionally the Rav would come downstairs to the YU cafeteria for lunch. (I was told that prior to his wife's passing away in 1967, the Rav and his wife would dine in the cafeteria regularly.) He would wait on line with his tray like anyone else. The students on line felt very uncomfortable about this and would leave the line in order to allow the Rav to move up to the checkout counter as quickly as possible. The Rav, however, was very adamant that all the students return to the line, and that he would wait his turn. He did not want to exploit his position at YU for personal gain.

I recall on one such occasion standing behind the Rav on line at the cafeteria. The YU cafeteria had three prices: for students, for staff members, and for outside guests. When the Rav approached the checkout counter, the checkout lady asked the Rav: "Sir, do you work here?" As the Rav nodded his head affirmatively, I interceded by informing the lady that if he didn't work here, none of us would be here either!

A similar story was told to me by the late President and Chancellor of Yeshiva University, R' Dr. Norman Lamm z"l. Beginning his tenure as President in 1976, R' Lamm felt that he should mingle with YU students in the cafeteria at lunchtime. He, too, waited on line with all the students. As he approached the checkout counter, the checkout lady, well acquainted with the various prices, asked this anonymous gentleman opposite her: "Sir, are you a student here?" To which R' Lamm responded: "No,

I'm no longer a student here." She continued: "Sir, do you teach here?" Pausing momentarily, R' Lamm answered: "No, I don't exactly teach here." "So," continued the lady, "are you a guest here?" Scratching his head, R' Lamm reacted: "No, I'm certainly not a guest here." At which point the very frustrated checkout lady concluded: "Sir, if you don't study here, and if you don't teach here, and you're not a guest here, then you're a nobody!!!!"

R' Lamm told me that he found this cafeteria conversation most humbling.

On another occasion, we learned an interesting Halakha from the Rav's actions in the cafeteria (מעשה רב). In the far corner of the cafeteria, a large group of students sat celebrating a *Sheva Berakhot* meal with a newly-married classmate. The group was at the point of *Birkat HaMazon* as the Rav entered the cafeteria. In spite of the fact that these YU students were not members of the Rav's *Shiur*, the Rav was asked by the group if he could join them for the reciting of the *Sheva Berakhot*. And, the Rav did just that. He recited all the *Sheva Berakhot* without partaking in the meal at all!

At the wedding of my son, Hayim, his high school *Rosh Yeshiva* arrived at the hall (after participating in four other weddings that evening!) at the very moment of *Birkat HaMazon*. In accordance with the Rav's precedent that I witnessed, we honored this *Rosh Yeshiva* with one of the *Sheva Berakhot*.

68

Returning a Nickel; Refunding Parking & Toll Fees

One day, in the middle of *Shiur* at YU, the Rav's ulcer began acting up. He turned to me and asked if I'd be kind enough to run down to the cafeteria and bring him a cup of milk. He gave me a quarter (25 cents) to pay. I ran as quickly as I could to the "caf" to bring the Rav his milk. It cost 30cents. I returned to the *Shiur* room with the cup of milk. The Rav took the cup, recited a *brakha*, drank the milk, and asked me how much it cost. I said: "It's okay." The Rav pressed: "So how much was it?" I said: "Not to worry, there's no change!" The Rav was still not satisfied. "How much did it cost?" he raised his voice. I said meekly: "30 cents." The Rav then said, "So, I owe you a nickel (5 cents)!" I said: "It's okay, I'm *moihel* (forgo) the five cents." I thought that the incident was behind me, until that afternoon, when the Rav uncharacteristically returned to the *Bet Midrash* flashing a nickel, asking: "Where is Adler?" When I came out to meet the Rav (and receive my nickel), I asked the Rav why he went to so much trouble to return a nickel to me. He looked at me and said: "Don't you know that there is a *din* (law) of *gezel* (theft) even on a *prutah* (smallest coin of value in the Talmudic era)." This incident made a deeper impression upon me than one hundred formal talks on business ethics.

This was also the reason that the Rav had a one-dollar bill prepared to give me every Tuesday morning at the weekly LaGuardia Airport pickup. Fifty cents was for the parking meter at the airport and another fifty cents for the toll at the

Tri-borough Bridge (Renamed: RFK Memorial Bridge). In spite of the fact that I would have been prepared to spend ten dollars for the opportunity to drive the Rav, he wouldn't allow this *hesed* (act of kindness) to drain me financially.

69

The Rav suffered throughout the years from two religious/psychological allergies. One was the printing press and the other was a סיום מסכת (a ceremony upon completion of a Talmudic tractate).

In the Rav's family, much was written, but very little printed in one's lifetime. The much-acclaimed novellae of the Rav's grandfather, R' Hayim *zt"l*, and uncle, R' Velvele *zt"l*, were all published posthumously by their children. A full-length book by the Rav (על התשובה) never appeared until he was nearly seventy years old. The feeling in the family was that as long as the mind is creative and dynamic, there's no need to freeze the ideas permanently in book form. This would only lead to the need to constantly issue updated editions. While alive and creative, there's no finality to Torah. After one's passing away, however, the net result is permanent and may go to press.

> Posthumously, there are over sixty books to date, published in different languages, that carry the Rav's name as the author. They include Biblical commentaries, *Shiurim* summaries, philosophical and social works.

For this very reason, the Rav was not an advocate of celebrating the end of a tractate or the end of a chapter of Talmud study. (In fact, the Rav did participate in such ceremonies when he felt that his absence would be a disappointment to the participants.) The impression created by such celebrations is that something has actually been completed. The point is that Torah can never be completed! The Rav would tell the story of his father, R' Moshe *zt"l*, the town Rabbi of Khaslovici, who refused the *Hatan Torah Aliya* on *Simhat Torah* completing the Torah reading cycle. But, he was happy to accept the *Hatan Bereishit Aliya*, commencing the new cycle of Torah reading. In all areas of Torah, one can always begin anew.

70   Epilogue - My Final Conversation (1985)

Six years had passed since my *Aliya* to Israel in 1979. My contact with the Rav during that time was marginal. I would write him letters keeping him up to date about my whereabouts and activities. It was important for me to inform him that I wasn't "lost" in Israel as he had feared (see Conversation #36). In 1981, when appointed to my first Israeli rabbinic position at the Young Israel of Beersheva, I asked the Rav to intercede on my behalf by recommending me to the Chief Rabbi of Israel, R' Shlomo Goren *zt"l*, in order to be certified as a community rabbi. The Rav did so graciously, and his letter assisted me immensely at that time.

In the summer of 1985, on a brief visit to the United States, I was able to attend the Rav's last RCA-sponsored *Yarhei Kallah* (a two-day learning marathon) in Boston. It was clear to all that the Rav's physical and mental health was failing. Nevertheless, there were moments of lucidity and brilliance even as the sun was setting on this unusual human being. The Rav, at that time, reacted to the criminal actions of the "Jewish Underground" group (מחתרת יהודית) who killed and murdered Palestinians. The Rav said that in the *Yom Kippur* listing of sins (על חטא), there are many sins mentioned from which most Jews are far removed. So, why bother confessing over them? The answer, explained the Rav, was that on *Yom Kippur* we confess for not only those sins actually committed, but also for the fleeting thought of perhaps committing a particular sin. On *Yom Kippur*, the slate must be completely clean.[17] Yet, there is one sin conspicuously absent from the list. This is the sin of murder. The reason is that should a Jew have the faintest desire to kill another individual, it would diminish his sanctity as a Jew (קדושת ישראל). Unfortunately, he noted, there are those in *Eretz Yisrael* today whose sanctity has been deminished.

At this occasion it was reported to me by R' Fabian Schonfeld *z"l*, illustrious Rabbi of the Young Israel of Kew Gardens Hills, Queens, NY, that the Rav had just advised the RCA leadership to adopt the opinion of Israel's Chief Rabbinate regarding the Jewish status of the Ethiopian immigrants. This included a de facto recognition of the Jewish background of this age-old community, along with the requirement of a conversion procedure diplomatically referred to in Israel as "התחדשות הברית" (renewing the covenant). This requirement was enacted in order to offset issues of *mamzeirut* in the family. On such public issues in Israel, the Chief Rabbis enjoy the status of מרא דאתרא. (See Conversation #37.)

I shed tears as I parted with the Rav for the final time. With all his memory lapses at that time, he still recalled who I was, and told me to send his best regards to all his friends in Beersheva. Wow! He remembered that I was in Beersheva! I cried.

The Rav passed away on *Hol HaMo'ed Pesah* of 1993 as the sun was setting after the seventeenth of Nissan. (The cemetery monument in Boston reads "the eighteenth of Nissan.")

In 1995, I had my first opportunity to visit the Rav's gravesite. (See Conversation #11). Members of one of the most loyal friends of the Rav, the Abelow family, accompanied me to Boston's West Roxbury cemetery. At that time, a new Junior and Senior Yeshiva high school was in formation in the Hashmona'im settlement in Israel. As the Founding *Rosh Yeshiva*, I wanted to perpetuate the Rav's name through my Yeshiva in Israel, and here was the golden opportunity. I took the cue from R' Meir Shapiro *zt"l*, founder of the Yeshiva Hakhmei Lublin in Poland, who visited

17. Rambam, *Hilkhot Teshuva* 2:7.

174

the gravesites of the sixteenth-century "Hakhmei Lublin" ("The Wise Men of Lublin," referring to R' Shlomo Luria – the MaHarSHaL, R' Shalom Shachne and others) asking them permission to name his twentieth century Yeshiva by that name: "Hakhmei Lublin." He obviously "heard" a positive response from the group. As mystical as this sounds, I, too, asked the Rav for his permission to name the newly-established Yeshiva in Hashmona'im in his memory, pledging to carry out, to the best of my ability, his Torah doctrines and teachings. I, too, "heard" a positive response. And so, with the encouragement and blessings of both the Twersky and Lichtenstein families, the Yeshiva was named (as suggested by R' Moshe Lichtenstein) "Yeshivat Ner Tamid." The acryonym "Tamid" spells out: תורת מורנו יוסף דב.

Through this Yeshiva, and through the teaching of Torah by hundreds of the Rav's students in Israel today, along with the immense popularity in Israel of the Rav's literary legacy, one can be consoled by the fact that the Rav finally did make it to *Eretz Yisrael*, albeit posthumously, in fulfillment of his lifelong dream.

יהי זכרו של מו"ר הגרי"ד הלוי סולוביצ'יק ברוך לעד

Accompanying the Rav, 1976. (*Photo: R'Aharon Ziegler*)

Postscript

As mentioned in the Preface, the framework of these seventy edited conversations with the Rav was predominantly the chauffeuring of the Rav during his weekly stay in New York City. In a 1957 public address to the merged Mizrahi / HaPoel HaMizrahi organization, the Rav articulated his feelings of flying to New York and his arrival at the Yeshiva.[1] The Rav's own words would best serve as the most fitting conclusion to the tales of ויהי בנסוע הארון.

> I am only a guest in New York. I regularly fly back and forth from Boston to New York. While aboard the plane I am often overwhelmed by the achievements of modern technology. The speed and exactness of the flight of the aircraft exemplify these accomplishments.
>
> At times, when observing these technological strides, I feel lost as I fly between the heavens and the earth. Man loses his independence, and I feel like a worthless object in the vastness of the universe. "When I behold Thy heavens, the work of Thy fingers ... what is man, that Thou are mindful of him? And the son of man, that Thou thinkest of him?" [Psalms 8:4–5]
>
> After the plane lands at LaGuardia Airport, I go directly to the Yeshiva. I immediately enter the world of Abaye and Raba. If you should ask how I feel with the sudden change in my environs when I enter the Yeshiva, I will respond that it is a superb transition. When I enter the world in which the same topics are discussed that were analyzed

1. *The Rav*, ed. R' Aaron Rakefet-Rothkoff, Vol. 2, 1999, pp. 224–225.

in the academies of Sura and Pumpeditha [in ancient Babylonia], I know that I am on firm and stable ground. In such endeavors there is perpetual truth. In the Yeshiva I am at home because I am grounded in the world of eternity.

About the Author

Rabbi Dr. Aaron Adler is a former student of, and special assistant to, Rabbi Joseph B. Soloveitchik, *zt"l*. In addition to being a graduate of Yeshiva University in New York (B.A./M.A), with rabbinic ordination from Y.U.'s Rabbi Isaac Elchanan Theological Seminary (R.I.E.T.S.), R' Adler holds a Ph.D in Talmud from Bar Ilan University.

R' Adler and his family made *aliyah* in 1979. He served on the faculty of Bar Ilan University, and is a past president and campus rabbi at Emunah College for Arts and Technology in Jerusalem. He has been a lecturer for the Israel Defense Forces and a commentator for Kol Yisrael radio. R' Adler was a member of the central committee of the National Religious Party. He is the founding Rosh Yeshiva of Yeshivat Bnei Akiva Ner Tamid, located in Hashmona'im, and currently serves as its President. R' Adler is an active community pulpit rabbi serving communities during the past 36 years in Long Island City, NY, Beersheva, Ramot-Jerusalem, Zurich-Switzerland, and most recently the Ohel Nechama community Synagogue in Katamon-Jerusalem. His current educational activities include: Lecturer at the Herzog College, OU Israel Center, Beit Tuvei Ha'ir, and the Kollel Sinai. Most recently, R' Adler has joined the faculty of the Bet Midrash Harel (*Semikha*-granting institution) focusing upon modern practical Halakha – methodology and application.

R' Adler is a popular scholar-in-residence both in Israel and throughout the world. He has also organized and led over 30 Jewish-heritage tours to Poland, Lithuania, and Belarus.